# The House
# That GOD Built

# The House
# That GOD Built

*Dr. Mark Hanby*

**Destiny Image® Publishers, Inc.**
**P.O. Box 310**
**Shippensburg, PA 17257-0310**

"Speaking to the Purposes
of God for this Generation"

ISBN 1-56043-091-5

For Worldwide Distribution
Printed in the U.S.A.

Third Printing: 1998          Fourth Printing: 1998

This book and all other Destiny Image, Revival Press,
and Treasure House books are available
at Christian bookstores and distributors worldwide.

For a U.S. bookstore nearest you, call **1-800-722-6774**.
For more information on foreign distributors, call **717-532-3040**.
Or reach us on the Internet: **http://www.reapernet.com**

# *Dedication*

*This book is lovingly dedicated to the covenant family in Chattanooga, Tennessee, who inspired and patiently endured the unfolding of the vision of the "House that God built."*

# *Contents*

# Chapter 1

# *Introduction*
# *"The House That God Built"*

The Christian Church of the nineties is drowning in a flood of human ideas and programs to bring "God's dreams" to pass. Impatient to impress, we preach on television each week, and our radio programs air three times a day. We knock on every door in town, run full-page advertisements in the newspaper, and our full-color billboards blanket every major highway.

An endless parade of guest preachers and singers compete for our pulpits and the chance to entertain bloated, infantile believers with an acquired taste for shallow, uncommitted Christianity. Meanwhile, millions are dying of spiritual hunger and thirst outside our bannered walls.

We promote popular spirituality and synthetic sincerity to the point where our members dance gaily from one congregation to the next, nibbling daintily at the latest religious smorgasbord of unanointed presentations and powerless pageantry. *Somehow, we're missing the mark.*

As a boy growing up on a comfortable little farm nestled in the Hocking Hills of Southeastern Ohio, I entered a new world of opportunity the day a gentleman gave me a bow and some arrows. The bow was only made of lemon wood and the arrows were less than professional, but that didn't bother me. I strutted all over the farm shooting at "stuff." I shot at haystacks, stumps, roots, rabbits, squirrels, and even chickens. They were all safe, however, because I couldn't hit anything.

When I finally realized that my performance wasn't measuring up to my expectations, I drew a target on a piece of cardboard and put it up on a bale of hay. After some practice shots and a minute or two of real thinking, I discovered that I could aim right at the target and still manage to put my arrow up in the limbs of a tree one time, and hit the ground in front of me the next! I couldn't understand how I could aim the point of that arrow at that target and still not hit it.

Things were looking bad for Robin Hood of Ohio until a friend came along and offered me a little advice: "Hey, Mark. I know you are pointing the arrow at the target, but you have no consistency in your 'knocking point'." (*What is a "knocking point?"* I wondered.) My friend explained to me that there is a place in the middle of the string where the force that thrusts the arrow is the strongest. There has to be a consistent point or mark on that string that keeps the arrow lined up straight.

As I grew older and moved up to the more powerful recurve and compound-type bows, I began to learn that there are certain things about archery that you don't consciously think about—things that are constant. They are already ordered, set, and established. For example, that arrow had to go on the string at exactly the same place *every time* if I expected to have any accuracy and consistency. I learned to hold the bow out at my side to make sure the arrow was level. Then I wrapped thread around the bowstring to mark the spot where the arrow was perfectly *aligned*. Once I discovered and marked this "knocking point," I was able to "knock" the arrow into proper position on the string every time.

My learning didn't stop there. Someone else explained to me that even though an arrow is "knocked" at the key place every time, it still may not be properly aligned. I learned that there had to be an "anchor" point as well as a "knocking" point. Some archers put their thumb behind their ear when they pull the string back to "anchor" their shot. Others put their index finger under their chin. I learned to draw the string and bring one of my fingers to the corner of my mouth. I was amazed at my progress! Aiming at the target and hitting it suddenly seemed like a simple procedure *as long as everything else was in order!*

Although our arrows all seem to be aimed in the right direction in our Christian lives and ministries, something is obviously out of order.

Ask any pastor, church leader, or minister, "What is your vision?" Without exception, they will immediately list all the goals they want to accomplish.

I'm going to reach this city.
We are going to preach around the world.
We're going to turn this nation around!
We want to see signs, wonders, and miracles.
Harvest is coming in our city.
God has given us prophecies, telling us that He has opened the windows of Heaven.
This is God's valley....

Of course these statements line up with the purposes and results of the gospel, but as I listen to these statements from pastors and leaders across the nation, I wonder why we see so little accomplishment. If you typed or wrote down all the prophecies received in some of our churches, you could paper the walls of the building! If these promises were made of carpet, you could cover the parking lot with them. The struggle and frustration of it all is that while we constantly claim and target these lofty goals, we are just not seeing the results they should produce.

Yes, we are aiming our arrows at the right targets. God's people aren't talking about wrong things. In fact, I generally sense pure desire in the men and women of God I meet around the country. Their hearts are honest and they really do care; many of them live in real stress and anguish because of their desire to see their visions accomplished. Consequently, we often get sidetracked and impatient, inventing a flood of human ideas to bring our dreams to pass. What if God were to take away from the Church everything He never told us to do? David wanted to build God a house, but the Lord had a totally different idea—"*I am going to build you a house!*" David's desires were good and his goals seemed right, but he learned that this was not *God's order*—the Lord had a totally different idea..."I am going to build you a house!" Thus was born the theme of this book, "The House That God Built."

Since then, I've been amazed to see how much *religion* we've managed to heap onto God's simple plan. We, like Martha, are "cumbered about much *serving*," and we are "careful and troubled about many things" (Lk. 10:40-41).

The apostle Paul was deeply concerned that the Corinthian church would be "corrupted from the *simplicity* that is in Christ" (2 Cor. 11:3). Have we become so busy with "our houses" that we've lost our focus and singleness of heart? What if, in the busy traffic of our "churchy activities," we have really lost sight of Him?

I believe this is why the apostle Paul wrote, "...but this *one* thing I do..." (Phil. 3:13). We promote and practice so many inconsistent ideas and programs in our "houses" that it's practically impossible for us to strike anywhere near the target of God's true Kingdom purpose! Our aim and direction in the "house" has to become so consistent and so spiritually instinctive that we don't have to think or worry about it.

It's like driving an automobile. When we first started driving, everything was critical. "How far do I turn the wheel, and how hard do I push on the gas pedal?" After a while, the whole process became second nature, it became a smooth, almost unconscious process. We didn't think about it anymore. There is an order or process in the Spirit that we must absorb, almost as a new spiritual instinct—without it, we will be forever shooting at the moon and hitting the ground. I became a much better archer once I learned that the target can be variable, but the "knocking point" and the "anchor point" have to be constant.

God wants to focus us; He wants to *bring us into alignment* in our settings, in our houses, and in our ministries. The vision is our target, but God's *order* for His house must become defined and automatic in us.

If you were to ask the apostle Paul, "What is your vision? What do you want more than anything for the Kingdom?" his reply would probably be, "I want a *real* relationship with Christ! Whatever it takes, I want to *"know Him"* (Phil. 3:10).

Everything in Paul's unequaled life of ministry was simply *the result of* his single-minded passion for Christ—he turned both the Jewish and gentile worlds upside down, he preached to all of Asia and virtually all of the known world. This man stood before the world's most powerful kings and authorities to testify of his love and devotion to Christ. He wrote epistles to all the churches that he had founded, producing more than one half of our New Testament in the process—all as a result of his sold-out relationship with Jesus Christ. Relationship and alignment with Christ was to Paul the "knocking point" and the "anchor point" of his life and ministry. It was the one constant around which everything else revolved. Everything else was merely the result or product of this dynamic relationship.

Spiritual relationships are vitally important to our purpose in life. In our relationship with the Lord Jesus, we are expected to reproduce Christ in the earth. Paul continually prayed for his spiritual children, and wrote to the believers in Galatia, "...of whom I travail in birth again until Christ be formed in you" (Gal. 4:19). If Christ is to be formed in us, and if there is to be a birthing of anointed things among us, it will be the product of proper relationship. When a healthy father and mother come into proper relationship, they rarely have to *try* to have children. In fact, the fruitfulness of their proper relationship can produce a different kind of problem—they have to be careful *not* to produce more offspring than they can properly raise. Children and reproduction are the natural product of proper relationship in a marriage.

In the same way, reproduction and fruitfulness are the natural (or *supernatural*) product of proper relationships in the Kingdom of God. Our lofty Kingdom goals of reaching towns, cities, nations, and the world shouldn't be seen as *our causes and goals*, so much as they should be the *supernatural result* of proper spiritual relationship, order, and alignment. All too often, we focus on the result instead of on the reason for a thing. If we can discover *God's way* of doing a thing, if we can discern the consistent spiritual order He wants us to observe in our lives and ministry, then we won't have to spend so much time struggling. The key to God's spiritual order is revealed in *The House That God Built.*

Although many are content simply to admire the grandeur of Solomon's temple (the land, the multi-purpose buildings, the wonderful programs, and dazzling promotions), God is solemnly calling us to come up, to enter the gates of His true house. It is here that we will discover—and learn to live out in practical ways—*the spiritual order* of the house that God built for David...and of *the house that God is building* in and with us!

# Chapter 2

# *The House of David*

*And it came to pass, when the king sat in his house, and the Lord had given him rest round about from all his enemies;*

*That the king said unto Nathan the prophet, See now, I dwell in an house of cedar, but the ark of God dwelleth within curtains.*

*And Nathan said to the king, Go, do all that is in thine heart; for the Lord is with thee.*

*And it came to pass that night, that the word of the Lord came unto Nathan, saying,*

*Go and tell My servant David, Thus saith the Lord, Shalt thou build Me an house for Me to dwell in?*

*Whereas I have not dwelt in any house since the time that I brought up the children of Israel out of Egypt, even to this day, but have walked in a tent and in a tabernacle.*

*In all the places wherein I have walked with all the children of Israel spake I a word with any of the tribes of Israel, whom I commanded to feed My people Israel, saying, Why build ye not Me an house of cedar?*

*Now therefore so shalt thou say unto My servant David, Thus saith the Lord of hosts, I took thee from the sheepcote, from following the sheep, to be ruler over My people, over Israel:*

*And I was with thee whithersoever thou wentest, and have cut off all thine enemies out of thy sight, and have made thee a great name, like unto the name of the great men that are in the earth.*

*Moreover I will appoint a place for My people Israel, and will plant them, that they may dwell in a place of their own, and move no more; neither shall the children of wickedness afflict them any more, as beforetime,*

*And as since the time that I commanded judges to be over My people Israel, and have caused thee to rest from all thine enemies. Also the Lord telleth thee that* He will make thee an house.

2 Samuel 7:1-11

*According to all these words, and according to all this vision, so did Nathan speak unto David.*

*Then went king David in, and sat before the Lord, and he said, Who am I, O Lord God? and what is my house, that thou hast brought me hitherto?*

2 Samuel 7:17-18

*And now, O Lord God, the word that Thou hast spoken concerning Thy servant, and concerning his house, establish it for ever, and do as Thou hast said.*

*And let Thy name be magnified for ever, saying, The Lord of hosts is the God over Israel: and let the house of Thy servant David be established before Thee.*

*For Thou, O Lord of hosts, God of Israel, hast revealed to Thy servant, saying,* I will build thee an house: *therefore hath Thy servant found in his heart to pray this prayer unto Thee.*

*And now, O Lord God, Thou art that God, and Thy words be true, and Thou hast promised this goodness unto Thy servant:*

*Therefore now let it please Thee to bless the house of Thy servant, that it may continue for ever before Thee: for Thou, O Lord God, hast spoken it: and with Thy blessing* let the house of Thy servant be blessed for ever.

2 Samuel 7:25-29

It is obvious by the reading of this chapter that David had an intense desire to build God a house...a place for God to dwell. It appears that David's thoughts and desires were honest and that his motive was absolutely pure.

There seems to be no hidden agenda in David's observation... "I dwell in a house of cedar...the ark of God dwelleth within curtains." The message rings clear; the purpose is plain. "I should not be personally blessed while God is struggling. Why should I have a definite place of rest while God is constantly moving?" Ah! What is the real point? While David has a pure heart and an untainted desire, it does not necessarily mean that God is requiring or desiring this permanent new house, or even accepting the creation of it. God is a moving thing!

God loved the tabernacle (2 Sam. 7:6). The Lord could throw up a little "cloud by day" and move. He could ignite a "pillar of fire" by night and set off...He is a moving thing.

The first time we ever see God in His Word, He is moving..."In the beginning God created the heaven and the earth. And the earth was without form, and void; and darkness was upon the face of the deep. And the Spirit of God

**moved** upon the face of the waters" (Gen. 1:1-2). The last time we see Divinity in Scripture, He is coming. "He which testifieth these things saith, Surely I come quickly. Amen. Even so, come, Lord Jesus" (Rev. 22:20).

Between the "goings" and the "comings" of the Lord, the Bible says "For as many as are **led** by the Spirit of God, they are the sons of God" (Rom. 8:14).

God loved the tent—He is a moving thing!

It is unique that David's desire came upon him in a certain mind-set, a particular type of situation. Scripture states that God had given David rest from his enemies round about (2 Sam. 7:1). He had entered into a certain "rest." He was not disturbed by the beating, banging and excessive clamor of battle. This also seems right. Getting his mind off personal warfare, he was better able to focus on God and his purpose. His ideas were creative and his passions were spiritual. Still, this does not necessarily constitute confirmation concerning his desire. While everything seemed right, God was not necessarily pleased.

David's desire was so intense that he rushed to the prophet Nathan and inquired of the Lord through him. This also seems accurate. David talked with a spiritual man about his "vision," and by the way, his vision received great acceptance in Nathan's heart.

His conversation might have gone something like this... "Brother Nathan, I was sitting in the house this evening thinking about the Lord. I looked at all the splendor of my house and thought, *How blessed I am.* And then I looked out of my window and was smitten with what I saw...the God who delivered me out of the paw of the bear, the jaw of the lion, the sword of Goliath and the armies of all my enemies is living in a **TENT**! Nathan, this is the God who gave me courage through those 15 long years from the oil in my father's back yard in Bethlehem to the gold in Hebron...I want to do something for God!"

I see David's desire in the hearts of ministers and church people everywhere I go. Pastors, teachers, workers—they all want to do something for God. No, these are not the spastic motions of new spiritual babes, of immature men and women in the Church. No one can convince me that these desires are just the overwrought feelings of flaky teachers hungry for personal gain and success. These people have a God-given, innate desire to see the Kingdom of God "come in the earth."

It has also become clear to me and to others that the "off-spring" of our honest, sincere desires does not always line up with the purpose and will of God. We have sired multitudes of programs and projects that often have nothing to do with what God is saying! We struggle on and on, outside of grace, to complete and accomplish meaningless ends to misguided projects—usually with the best of motives and intentions.

Even though Nathan confirmed David's feelings about building God a house, the Lord spoke to him in the night and said, "Go tell My servant David, thus saith the Lord, shalt thou build Me a house for Me to dwell in?" In other words, God asked, "Did I tell you to do this?" The answer is obviously NO!

The tenth and eleventh verses of the seventh chapter finally let us in on the holy secret. We more clearly see the mind and purpose of God! In essence it says—"I never told you to build Me a house. I said that I would **build you a**

**house**, David, and give you a Messiah for a son!" What a startling, striking revelation! **God wanted to build His own house!**

Later in retrospect, Solomon prayed this truth: "And it was in the heart of David my father to build an house for the name of the Lord God of Israel. And the Lord said unto David my father, Whereas it was in thine heart to build an house unto My name, thou didst well that it was in thine heart. Nevertheless thou shalt not build the house..." (1 Kings 8:17-19a). "And now, O God of Israel, let Thy word, I pray Thee, be verified, which Thou spakest unto Thy servant David my father. But will God indeed dwell on the earth? behold, the heaven and heaven of heavens cannot contain Thee; how much less this house that I have builded?" (1 Kings 8:26-27)

Now the passage in Psalm 127:1 takes on precious meaning..."Except the Lord build the house, they labor in vain that build it..."

It seems I hear David's son in possessive deification proclaim...Upon this Rock **I will build My church**! (Mt. 16:18) So in fact, the "House of David" that we are talking about in this book is not a house that David built at all. It is a house...a place...an order established by God Himself. One theologian states that God gave David a "window in the dispensation through which he could see all things in Christ and the Church."

This is not a physical house. There is no tangible structure to this building. From this point and forward through the Scriptures, we begin seeing the unfolding revelation of spiritual order and alignment which becomes the constant habitation of the Spirit in every age, to every people.

Zechariah said that a fountain would be opened in the house of David (Zech. 12:10; 13:1). Zacharias, the father of John the Baptist, prophesied that this Christ was literally the Salvation brought forth in the house of David (Lk. 1:68-69).

Peter preached David's house and throne at Pentecost (Acts 2:29-36). James settled the New Testament church dispute (Acts 15:16-18) by claiming the Gentiles' salvation was the rebuilding of David's house. The glorified Jesus, standing in the middle of the seven golden candlesticks, claimed that the Philadelphian church had..."an open door" and that it had been opened with the "Key of David!" (Rev. 3:7).

There is another extremely important aspect of the building of God's house. David could not build God's house because he was a man of war...his hands had shed blood (1 Chron. 22:6-8). He belonged to the days of labor. Solomon, David's son, was allowed to build a physical house in David's stead (2 Sam. 7:12-13). Do you realize that Solomon is the *third* in the line of Jewish kings?

Saul represented the *First Dimension*, associated with the bloody works of the outer court of God's tabernacle. David represented the *Second Dimension* of the tabernacle, bringing oil for light, bread for the table, and sweet incense (praise) for the golden altar. Here we see a mixture of flesh and spirit, where bloody hands ministered to God and His people under the anointing and grace of God. But David could not go beyond that invisible line symbolized by the bounds of the Holy Place in the tabernacle. David could not enter into God's rest beyond the veil, or ask God to reside where bloody hands had defiled His resting place.

Only Solomon was able to "enter into rest" in the *Third Dimension.* Solomon's function represents the third king, the third and highest level of the tabernacle. It was this king who was allowed to build a tabernacle and invite God to arise to His resting place in the Most Holy Place (2 Chron. 6:41-7:2).

The physical temple built by Solomon (which served as a temporary type or shadow of the eternal spiritual house of David) was built without the sound of a hammer or any other tool of iron (1 Kings 6:7). In other words, the physical building which became a type of God's true spiritual house was built in peace. There was no clamor there—struggle was unacceptable. The true house was built somewhere beyond warfare! In fact, the stones for Solomon's temple were cut and fashioned perfectly *before* they were put in place at the temple site! What does this say about the *lively stones* the Master Builder uses to build His house (1 Pet. 2:5)?

Even the priests of God in the Old Testament, in pattern under Moses and Aaron, could not wear clothing against their bodies that caused them to sweat. The work of the ministry was to be done in a certain solace. The attitude of God's servants was to be that of rest and peace. This was the order of the house of God.

In the New Testament, we learn about a new day—a day of rest. "For if Jesus had given them rest, then would He not afterward have spoken of another day. There remaineth therefore a rest to the people of God. For he that is entered into his rest, he also hath ceased from his own works, as God did from His" (Heb. 4:8-10).

Of course, when we start talking about "the seventh day" or "the third day" of grace...all the dispensationalists begin quoting their practiced eschatologies, reminding us that we must tarry for the "times."

Consider the possibility, however, that we may not have to wait for the ages to mature in order to receive ultimate promises. Time only marks the passing of our mortality. God lives in eternity. If Adam had not sinned, time would have been totally insignificant to His everlastingness.

In John chapter seventeen, Jesus literally transcends time in his reconciliatory prayer in the garden of Gethsemane! He made statements like..."I am no longer in the world"...while frankly, He was right there in the garden. Moving out of the temporal and into the eternal, He reached back in time and said..."Glorify Thou Me...with the glory that I had before the world was." Reaching ahead, He proclaimed that He had..."finished the work" that His Father had sent Him to do." There had not yet been a death, burial, or ressurection!

Beyond time, all things are **now** in God. It is always **today** (Heb. 3:13). In Christ all things are the same—yesterday, today and forever! (Heb. 13:8)

So we travel into the full purpose of God. We are not waiting for the year 2000 to move into this rest of the Third Dimension! *Today,* we are called to approach the inner place *behind the veil*—past the outer court (the First Dimension) and the Holy Place (Second Dimension), into the sovereign dwelling place where, through our proper order and alignment, God fulfills His purposes through us. God builds His house in the tabernacles of men from His resting place in the Third Dimension of Grace!

If the "house of David" described in Scripture is not a physical structure, then it is certainly **not** the temple of Solomon!

As we have stated before, David's house is a *spiritual order* reaching into every age and to every people.

The problem is that we have difficulty visualizing this house. It seems hidden, shrouded in mystery. Worse yet, it is swallowed up by a maze of religious endeavors, making the truth of its existence almost unidentifiable.

Do you remember the Key of David that opened the city door for the Philadelphian church? Isaiah declared that this key, in fact, opens the door to David's House! "And the key of the house of David will I lay upon His shoulder; so He shall open, and none shall shut; and He shall shut, and none shall open" (Is. 22:22).

Isn't it interesting that the glorified Christ said He had the key. More interesting, even blind beggars called Him "Son of David." And most interesting of all, the Scriptures state that in His final glory, Jesus will sit on the throne of His father, David.

We will seek Him—He alone holds the key! Ask satan! He knows he lost this key with all the others when Jesus brought back our inheritance, including a house—the house that God built.

# Chapter 3

# *Preparing the House*

*Then David said, This is the house of the Lord God, and this is the altar of the burnt offering for Israel.*

*And David commanded to gather together the strangers that were in the land of Israel; and he set masons to hew wrought stones to build the house of God.*

*And David prepared iron in abundance for the nails for the doors of the gates, and for the joinings; and brass in abundance without weight;*

*Also cedar trees in abundance: for the Zidonians and they of Tyre brought much cedar wood to David.*

*And David said, Solomon my son is young and tender, and the house that is to be builded for the Lord must be exceeding magnifical, of fame and of glory throughout all countries: I will therefore now make preparation for it. So David prepared abundantly before his death.*

1 Chronicles 22:1-5

This Scripture containing David's commands to prepare and gather material for the building of the Temple comes immediately following a very tragic episode in his life.

David was "provoked" by satan to number Israel (1 Chron. 21:1). Actually, he was tempted to measure the strength of

---

19

God's people by a physical means. He lapses in his great trust in God and seeks to determine the ability of his kingdom by assessing the number of its fighting men.

God was displeased with David's faithless action and immediately smote Israel with devastating judgment ..."and there fell of Israel seventy thousand men" (1 Chron. 21:14).

David and the elders of Israel clothed themselves in sackcloth and fell upon their faces. Of course, David repented, paid a dear price for a place to offer a sacrifice, built an altar and God mercifully stopped the awful plague. I have introduced this familiar story to show an often-overlooked sequence in the book of First Chronicles:

*At that time when David saw the Lord had answered him in the threshingfloor of Ornan the Jebusite, then he sacrificed there.*

*For the tabernacle of the Lord, which Moses made in the wilderness, and the altar of the burnt offering, were at that season in the high place at Gibeon.*

*But David could not go before it to inquire of God: for he was afraid because of the sword of the angel of the Lord.*

*Then David said,* This is the house of the Lord God, *and this is the altar of the burnt offering for Israel.*

*And David commanded to gather together the strangers that were in the land of Israel; and he set masons to hew wrought stones to build the house of God.*

*And David prepared iron in abundance for the nails for the doors of the gates, and for the joinings, and brass in abundance without weight:*

*Also cedar trees in abundance: for the Zidonians and they of Tyre brought much cedar wood to David.*

***And David said, Solomon my son is young and tender,
and the house that is to be builded for the Lord must be
exceeding magnifical, of fame and of glory throughout
all countries:*** I will therefore now make preparation

for it. *So David prepared abundantly before his death.*
1 Chronicles 21:28–22:5

I am intrigued by this catalog of "motives and makings." David gets into big trouble with God through personal disobedience and corporate mishandling. God "punishes David by bringing destruction to David's people"...his sheep.

Out of this catastrophe David unwittingly locates the unseen, invisible habitation of Deity. He claims that the threshingfloor of Ornan is really the "House of God." He located it through the process of his failure and repentance. If he had not "fallen," the tabernacle might forever have remained in a "high place" at Gibeon—out of reach and out of touch.

Next, the awful price paid out in human life due to his error, weighing like a millstone about his neck, summoned David to the immediate reconstruction of "God things." His tears washed his fading vision and caused him to clearly see a magnificent house where others saw only Ornan's barn.

Pain is an *absolute* in locating the progressive will of God. Without the pangs of death and suffering, ministries go on and on in hopeless confusion and worthless man-made projects. We build our "houses" in Gibeon because we've never caught the vision of the "City of David," complete with God's great house.

It is also noteworthy that David *prepared* to build the physical house only after he had, through suffering, caught a vision of the spiritual, invisible house.

I believe there is a pattern here—perhaps a misunderstood principle to be relearned. Failure and struggles are often the catalyst for change—change from old ideas and activities to new desires and purposes. Somewhere in this course of our self-fashioned ministries there must be a space for "losing our lives."

The first step, therefore, in preparing the real house may very well be the process of *death*. Whether self-inflicted or otherwise imposed, we must *die* if we are going to see the resurrection of the true house of God.

What if our efforts were confined only to preparing substance for those things we have already observed in the Spirit? We just might lose interest in bank accounts and auditoriums, numbers and a host of other manufactured flytraps to catch unsuspecting sinners. Somewhere beneath the surface of all our "man-things," God is lurking—waiting for us to capitulate so He can once again pull us back into pure vision and honest understanding. We must somehow learn, no matter how costly, that *all of our labor will never build a house for God*!

Let me here deal with the word "prepare." The first syllable, *pre-*, means "before, in advance of." The second syllable, *-pare*, means "to measure against." Another word that comes from the derivation is *par*, which means "a level, a mark, a line, or determined or stationary goal." That *par* is a "constant," something that doesn't move. In all of our highs and lows, there is a signal that does not vary. In all of melody, and in the wavelength of sound or voice, there is a certain line or *par* that cuts through—the stationary line of demarcation. It does not matter how high things are or how low things are...God has a way of bringing us down or up to par. This is Paul's "mark" of the "high calling of God in Christ Jesus" that he was pressing for (Phil. 3:14). To attain it, he was willing to suffer the "loss of all things" (Phil. 3:8). He also submitted to being conformed into the image of Christ, through suffering and resurrection!

I am reminded at this point, of old Simeon's prophecy concerning the child Jesus, recorded in the second chapter of the Gospel of Luke. Simeon had entered the temple at the precise moment when Joseph and Mary brought Jesus to be circumcised and added to the Jewish registry. Like a streaking linebacker, this old shuffling prophet intercepted the system, gathered up the Messiah in his arms, and prophesied concerning Him. Simeon's first statement was that the child, Jesus, would be "A light to lighten the Gentiles, and the glory of Thy people Israel" (Lk. 2:32).

The second dimension of this magnificent utterance stated that He, Jesus, would be "...set for the fall and rising again of many in Israel; and for a sign [mark] which shall be spoken against" (verse 34). The third dimension of Simeon's prophecy lets us know that Mary and Joseph (the origin of His flesh) would have a death—"a sword shall pierce through"—exposing the attitude of those nearby and judging their attitude concerning sufferings (verse 35). Notice the second phase of the prophecy: "...set for the fall and rise [in that order] again of many in Israel; and for a sign [line, mark] which shall be spoken against [measured against]" (verse 34). This is the "par" of the Spirit—the line to which all high things come down and all low things come up. This is the predetermined order of the house. This is God's opinion of what is right and worthy. John the Baptist would say, "Every valley shall be filled, and every mountain and hill shall be brought low..." (Lk. 3:5).

Somewhere beneath the obvious happenings of our practical procedures is the "God-thought-of" purpose for our greater usefulness. He alone knows what could be if all things were at a spiritual "par." He alone knows what the high water mark of our usefulness is. That is why Paul said "...I do not count myself to have apprehended [arrived]: but this *one* thing I do, forgetting [disregarding] those things which are behind, and reaching forth unto those things which are before, I press toward the *mark* [pre-pared] for the prize of the high calling of God in Christ Jesus." And then he further admonishes, "Let us therefore, as many as be perfect [mature, full grown, having suffered], be thus minded..." (Phil. 3:13-15). In other words, after you've been through all the struggles, why not let God establish (or reestablish) the goals of your life and ministry? Perhaps we should all begin, again, to find the "mark," the goal and purpose of our ministries!

Perhaps the spiritual passage into the fuller purpose of God is "death to self" and loss of the past. God wants to totally reprogram us to a whole new concept of trust and service.

Maybe the future depends on our preparation and not on our production. We constantly speak of faith in God. But perhaps we do not really need faith in the "product" (outcome of our labor), but rather faith in the process—that which is necessarily put upon us to bring about the true purpose of God in our lives.

When I totally lose the ambition to regulate spiritual happenings, and completely destroy all human advantages, I may very well be in proper position to see what God is doing in these last days.

Let us die to our ideas and self-ordinations. Let us demolish all personal distractions and human bargaining—and be baptized again and again with the spirit of self-denial until we are ready, again, to see the construction of God's house. We will gather and collect, we will assemble and prepare. But we will not *build* until we first see the unseen...the vision of the true *House that God built.*

# Chapter 4

# *The Order of the House*

*And he [Solomon] appointed, according to the order of David his father, the courses of the priests to their service, and the Levites to their charges, to praise and minister before the priests, as the duty of every day required: the porters also by their courses at every gate: for so had David the man of God commanded.*

*And they departed not from the commandment of the king [David] unto the priests, and the Levites concerning any matter, or concerning the treasures.*

*Now all the work of Solomon was prepared unto the day of the foundation of the house of the Lord, and until it was finished. So the house of the Lord was perfected.*

2 Chronicles 8:14-16

The physical construction of Solomon's Temple took more than fifteen years. One of the unique facts surrounding the temple project is that in all of those years, there was not heard the sound of a hammer or any other tool (1 Kings 6:7). This might not have been of great consequence if the structure had been simple, and the building cheaply assembled. On the contrary, archaeologists and historians tell us that the temple, with all of its profusion of gold, silver, precious stones, carved cedars and woven tapestries, was worth multiplied millions of dollars in our present currency. Furthermore, the temple's foundation and walls were built of huge stones, each weighing several tons—this was no "prefabbed" building. It was, however, a *prepared* "house." Every stone and article of the temple construction had been "pre-pared," shaped and fashioned through years of tedious preparation *before* they were placed in this glorious house. Everything was assembled in an *exact order*.

I think that it is also an interesting point that Solomon is nowhere to be found in the physical directorship of the building of the great temple. Shouldn't he at least be overseeing and approving the construction? According to Scripture, he was busy doing other things. He was studying the *order of his father David*! He is consumed with interest in the courses of the priests and how they serve—the Levites and their charges—the ministers and their service. Solomon is studying the duty of every day and what it requires.

How do you compare the work of the porter who "keeps the door" and the physical value of every gate? Were these duties trite compared to the cost of the furniture, or is this really the true essence of the order of the house? The Scriptures confirm Solomon's action by adding "for so had the man of God (David) commanded" (2 Chron. 8:14).

The Bible says, "Now all the work of Solomon was prepared unto the day of the foundation of the house of the Lord, and until it was finished. So the house of the Lord was perfected" (2 Chron. 8:16). In other words, even while craftsmen busily placed foundation stones and seated the carved cedar pillars, beams, and panels, and while skilled craftsmen put the finishing touches on the delicate gold furniture for the house, the house was still not completed or perfect without the established order of what to do in the house. This magnificent manifestation of human productivity is only the evidence of a greater house with spiritual bulwarks and unseen foundations. The *real* temple is Solomon's obsession. He realizes that the house that God is building is the spiritual order of what must be fulfilled within the temple.

The New Testament commands, "Let everything be done decently and in order" (1 Cor. 14:40). This, by the way, does not necessarily mean that children shouldn't run in the hall, or chew gum in church. The passage truly means that everything has an order and must be done in that order!

In the Tabernacle of Moses and the Temple of Solomon, there were several courts with corresponding furniture. These articles all had a specific place and position. The priests had certain activities and duties to perform at each of the furniture placements.

For example, the brazen altar was the place of the blood sacrifice; the laver, the place of washing and cleansing, etc. Each piece was in its place and attended in its order.

Psalm 122:1 begins, "I was glad when they said unto me, Let us go into the house of the Lord." The fifth verse continues, "For there are set thrones of judgment, the thrones of the house of David." This passage shines a powerful light on David's understanding of the "house." He recognized the differing positions of the furniture and the arrangement of courts to be "thrones" of judgment in the house.

A throne is not used for man to recline but rather for kings to rule. Each area of the true house brings you face to face with God's requirements and expectations with corresponding spiritual adjustment. Advancement from court to court depended solely upon the priests' submission in each preceding station. Thus the thrones were examination points to adjust the ascent of the ministers of the Lord as they progressed into the holy things of God.

God's Word teaches us that "judgment must begin at the house of God" (1 Pet. 4:17). There must be proper examination of our purpose and procedures, or we fall into the trap of practiced religion with little concern or evaluation of spiritual responsibilities. The house of God then becomes a sterile thing, with rulings and rituals, losing the true order of the spiritual house.

In later chapters, we will attempt to make the Word flesh by adding Christian practicum to the old type. We will name the furniture with its corresponding judgment or pattern for alignment. We will also attempt to understand and see the seven major positions of the tabernacle furniture as pillars of wisdom in our lives. According to Proverbs 9:1, these are the major structural undergirdings for the house. By the way, the text doesn't say the pillars are there in place, but rather that "Wisdom...hath hewn out her seven pillars." Submission to order has a way of carving away the excess and leaving us with only the necessary truths.

I feel at this point gently urged to launch into major discourses on theocracy, spiritual attributes, the five-fold ministry, and other key subjects, but I will resist the impulse in this overview chapter. These and more subjects will catch our direct attention in later chapters.

Let me go back now to Solomon and the temple that he has just completed. Remember, he knows that the true house is somewhere inside the temple—an order prepared by David which is far more important than the physical house.

He now prays the most magnificent prayer of all the Old Testament. His petition requests that if people are in trouble and look toward the "house," then they would get help. If they were at war with enemies surrounding them, that they could look toward the "house" and be delivered. If the heavens were to be shut up and no rain would come for the crops and harvest, they should be able to look toward the "house" and receive relief. If they sinned, Solomon prayed that the God in the house would forgive them; if they were carried away by their enemies into strange lands, and if they would look toward the "house," mercy would bring them back.

This awesome prayer consumes the entire sixth chapter of the Book of Second Chronicles. The last three verses, however, say as much as the other verses combined: "Now, my God, let, I beseech Thee, Thine eyes be open, and let Thine ears be attent unto the prayer that is made in this place" (verse 40).

I get the feeling that Solomon is indicating that although the literal building has geographical location, the true house may be transported spiritually to meet the people at the point of their need.

Verse 41 continues, "Now therefore arise, O Lord God, into Thy resting place, Thou, and the ark of Thy strength: let Thy priests, O Lord God, be clothed with salvation, and let Thy saints rejoice in goodness." In other words, Solomon is saying, "We've got a big, beautiful building here, Lord, but by the way—we need *You* to come in and reside here. We would really like for You to make this temple Your resting place. We've followed the order in construction...no struggles, no clamor, and no foolishness, but still—without Your presence—the natural order is hollow and dead. Oh, Lord

God, turn not away the face of Thine anointed: remember the mercies of David Thy servant. We've got the building, but You've got to build David's house."

"I've done all I can do," Solomon is saying. "Would You kindly remember Your promise to my father? If You don't build the true house, there will be nothing here but wood and stones and things...."

When Solomon finished his prayer, the Bible tells us that the glory of God filled the temple so that the priests could not enter into the house (2 Chron. 7:1-2). When the children of Israel saw the fire and the glory of God upon and inside the house, they fell on their faces and worshiped, saying, "For He is good; for His mercy endureth forever" (verse 3). This was not a response to the physical beauty of the temple, but rather, a holy reaction to viewing the *order* of the house producing glory in the house.

We can exist without physical structures and get by without personal conveniences, but we cannot live without the glory of God in our house.

# Chapter 5

# *The Vision of the House*

*And when the queen of Sheba heard of the fame of Solomon, she came to prove Solomon with hard questions at Jerusalem, with a very great company, and camels that bare spices, and gold in abundance, and precious stones: and when she was come to Solomon, she communed with him of all that was in her heart.*

*And Solomon told her all her questions: and there was nothing hid from Solomon which he told her not.*

*And when the queen of Sheba had seen the wisdom of Solomon, and the house that he had built,*

*And the meat of his table, and the sitting of his servants, and the attendance of his ministers, and their apparel; his cupbearers also, and their apparel; and his ascent by which he went up into the house of the Lord; there was no more spirit in her.*

*And she said to the king, It was a true report which I heard in mine own land of thine acts, and of thy wisdom;*

*Howbeit, I believed not their words, until I came, and mine eyes had seen it. And, behold, the one half of the greatness of thy wisdom was not told me; for thou exceedest the fame that I heard.*

*Happy are thy men, and happy are these thy servants, who stand continually before thee, and hear thy wisdom.*

*Blessed be the Lord thy God, who delighted in thee to set thee on His throne, to be king for the Lord thy God; because thy God loved Israel, to establish them forever, therefore made He thee king over them, to do judgment and justice.*

2 Chronicles 9:1-8

The queen of Sheba came from Arabia...beautiful radiant Arabia with its dike-watered pastures supporting fleecy flocks and shaded valleys with ancient old trees. She came from the land of silks, spices, and gold!

She had heard of the splendor of Solomon. Perhaps she thought to match her own wealth and wit with his.

The Scriptures state that she brought wealth with her—camels loaded with spices, gold in abundance, and bags of precious stones. She knew the life of luxury—"things" were of small consequence to her.

When she arrived in Jerusalem, her first interests were not of a temple or a house built for a god. "She communed," the Word says, with Solomon "...of all that was in her heart." Evidently she had many unanswered questions, and Solomon, wise as he was, told her all the answers. "...There was nothing hid from Solomon which he told her not."

Now it is time for a tour—the main purpose of her visit seems to be accomplished. She has seen the wisdom of Solomon and now she sees the temple.

I find it amusing that she did not praise the structure. She made no comment about the physical construction, the ornate decoration or the vast exhibition of wealth. Her attention was riveted on something else—"the sitting of his servants, and the attendance of his ministers...his cupbearers also, and their apparel." What do you really think she saw?

I believe she caught a vision of David's house—the one God built. Solomon's earthly construction paled in view of the real!

This heathen queen, looking past the form and the obvious, glimpsed the typical order of the Church and its theocratic government! The servants were the Levites—typical of the New Testament deacons—and they were happy! The ministers were the priests (New Testament elders). They were happy, there was a certain attitude about them—they had an apparel (covering) signifying that they were under authority and that there was no stress or competition among them. They served with willing hearts, all of them loving the wisdom of Solomon, typical of the Word of God!

This is the spiritual order of David's house—something far beyond the physical!

> *And he* [Solomon] *appointed, according to the order of David his father, the courses of the priests to their service, and the Levites to their charges, to praise and minister before the priests, as the duty of every day required: the porters also by their courses at every gate: for so had David the man of God commanded.*
>
> *And they departed not from the commandment of the king* [David] *unto the priests and Levites concerning any matter, or concerning the treasures.*
>
> *Now all the work of Solomon was prepared unto the day of the foundation of the house of the Lord, and until it was finished. So the house of the Lord was perfected.*
>
> 2 Chronicles 8:14-16

Was this house perfected by the gold, silver, carved cedar, curtains, or precious stones? No—it was perfected by the operation of the ministry within it!

Now, Solomon, with his ministry team, begins "his ascent by which he went up into the *house* of the Lord" (2 Chron. 9:4). This is where all resistance fled! No more questions, no more wonder, no more fear! The Word states, "...there was no more spirit in her."

How far could she really see? Maybe she could only see to the gate. As the singers and musicians worshiping Jehovah with the priests disappeared beyond the gates to offer the sacrifice, her own heart was lifted up. She may not have glimpsed the altar, laver, lampstand, tables of shewbread, altar of incense, and certainly not the ark of God's glory; but she saw something that melted her carnal resistance and ignited in her a feeling of the actual purpose. I believe she was glimpsing the other house. Upon beholding it, she gasped in awe—"You didn't tell me everything"..."the one half of the greatness of thy wisdom was not told me: for thou exceedest the fame that I heard (2 Chron. 9:6).

The other "half" was not really Solomon's wisdom at all; it was really the house that God was building for David and his royal seed. Looking far enough and long enough, the queen might have seen not only Solomon, but *another son of David in another day,* walking into a temple. His disciples had brought Him to "see the stones," the phenomenal foundational structure and bulwarks of Herod's Temple (a distant echo of Solomon's Temple). Upon viewing that wonder, Jesus startled His followers by stating, "A greater than Solomon is *here*" (Mt. 12:42). He really said, "The temple is actually in the temple," *the house that God built* is in the house! The tabernacle of God was truly "with men"...the Word was "made flesh"—the House was standing there speaking to them (Rev. 21:3, Jn. 12:42).

Jesus further incited the wrath of His pious religious enemies by exclaiming that what the ages had not eroded nor effaced, He could destroy and completely rebuild in three days (Jn. 2:19-20). Their groggy minds, polluted by the grandeur of man's production and sick with the fermentation of religious politics, accused Him of threatening their hallowed system and its artifices. These blind teachers could never have understood that He "spake of the temple of His body!" (verse 21). He was the true house—the fullness of God's glory was in Christ!

Certainly this heathen queen wouldn't have glimpsed what Jesus' own disciples didn't see after following and hearing Him for more than three years as He tried to open their sleepy spiritual eyes to the still greater vision of the house.

This other son of David, the Son of God, sounds much like the original temple builder when He uses the words: "Father's house" and "prepare." In John 14:1-3, Jesus said, "Let not your heart be troubled: ye believe in God, believe also in Me. In My Father's house [there it is!] are many *mansions*; [*monai*, the Greek word meaning *bodies or permanent dwelling places*] if it were not so, I would have told you. I go to prepare [there it is again!] a place for you. And if I go and prepare a place [a permanent dwelling place] for you, I will come again, and receive you unto Myself. That where I am [or what I am] there ye may be also!"

Now again, our past dispensational viewpoint places all this in the glory world, post-rapture, and beyond mortal reach. Consider the further information given by Jesus to these struggling followers who, by the way, also didn't know where He was going, or the "why" of His going in verse 5. He explains that they are about to personally receive another Comforter (Rest), who would abide with them forever—"...even the Spirit of Truth which the world could not receive." This was because the world could not SEE Him (no vision), and it certainly didn't know who or what He was (verse 16). He goes on to say, "but ye know Him: for He dwelleth with you [Jesus], and shall be *in you.*" *I will not leave you comfortless, I* [Jesus] *will come to you!* Wow! That explains His return (verse 3) to take them to where He was—He would return in another way (form) and they would become *His dwelling place!* He, remember, is the door to the real house!

*Seeing Him,* seems to be at issue here. They must have had a vision of Him that the world could not receive (verse 17). This adds a possible variation to our understanding of Colossians chapter three: "...If ye then be risen with Christ, seek those things which are above, where Christ sitteth on the right hand of God. Set your affections on things above [the house] not on things on the earth. For ye are dead and your life is hid with Christ in God. When Christ who is our life shall *appear* [be seen] then shall ye also appear with Him in glory" (Col. 3:1-4). That sounds a lot like First John 3:2— "Beloved now are *we* the sons of God and it doth not yet *appear* what we shall be, but we know that, when he shall *appear* [be seen] we shall be like Him; for we shall *see Him* as He is."

The apostle Paul repeatedly makes the point that *something,* some *mystery,* has already been delivered to us. This mystery is tied closely to God's glory and riches. He wrote:

*...I am made a minister, according to the dispensation of God which is given to me for you, to fulfil the word of God;*

*Even the mystery which hath been hid from ages and from generations, but now is made manifest to His saints:*

*To whom God would make known what is the riches of the glory of this mystery* [not a physical temple] *among the Gentiles; which is Christ in you, the hope of glory.*

Colossians 1:25-27

Are we going too far with this "seeing" or vision thing if we include a portion of Paul's manifesto to the mystery of the New Covenant? "Seeing then that we have such hope, we use great plainness of speech: and not as Moses, which put a vail over his face, that the children of Israel could not stedfastly look to the end of that which is abolished: but their minds were *blinded*: for until this day remaineth the same veil untaken away in the reading of the old testament; *which veil is done away in Christ*" (2 Cor. 3:12-14). The great apostle states that we all really become what we behold. We must see Glory to produce Glory—if we do not catch a vision of the true tabernacle in its deepest dimension, we can never fill the earth with the Glory of God.

Paul further states, "For our light affliction, which is but for a moment, worketh for us a far more exceeding and eternal weight of glory! While we *LOOK* [see] not at the things that which are seen [Solomon's Temple] but at the things which are not seen..." (2 Cor. 4:17-18).

The eloquent writer of the Epistle to the Hebrews states:

**But we see Jesus, *who was made a little lower than the angels for the suffering of death, crowned with glory***

*and honor; that He by the grace of God should taste death for every man.*

*For it became Him, for whom are all things, and by whom are all things, in bringing many sons unto glory, to make the* Captain *of their salvation perfect through sufferings.*

*For both He that sanctifieth and they who are sanctified are all of one: for which cause He is not ashamed to call them brethren,*

Hebrews 2:9-11

Look closely at the last verse again: "For both He that sanctifieth and they who are sanctified are *all of one*: for which cause He is not ashamed to call them brethren." *We become what He is when we see Him.*

Finally I want to remind us of Solomon's warning in Proverbs 29:18. "Where there is no vision, the people perish...." This verse is certainly not speaking of the people of the world, but rather of the people of God who do not understand the "heart matters," the real issues of life. And the explanation might be, "Without a progressive spiritual revelation, the people dwell carelessly."

The lackadaisical "Who cares?" attitude manifested by many Christians today is a testimony to their loss of vision and relationship with the real house, Jesus Christ.

Paul's "hope of glory" passage is followed immediately by "warning every man" (Col. 1:27-28). His "glory to glory" passage is followed by "renounced the hidden things of dishonesty, not walking in craftiness, nor handling the Word of God deceitfully" (2 Cor. 3:18;4:2).

His "far more exceeding and eternal weight of glory" passage is connected to "affliction" and the "perishing of the outward man" (2 Cor. 4:16-17). The "bringing many sons into glory" passage is the result of "suffering" and "sanctification" (Heb. 2:10-11). Everything is spent to reach the "glory." We might say that *reaching the ark in the Holiest place is worth visiting all the altars of the outer court.* The house that God is building is often denied because its construction requires our self-denial. Since we, in fact, become the "living stones" for the real tabernacle (1 Pet. 2:5), the hewing and shaping is often rejected for easier religious methods of structuring.

We can spiritualize all day and fill volumes with suppositions and pre-moralized information, but perhaps we should go back again and simply begin to walk through the tabernacle. We will move progressively, step by step, throne by throne, pillar by pillar.

Let us not linger at the building stones of information produced by scores of scholars, who thankfully have shared their studies to help us see the redemptive work of Christ typified and illustrated in the arrangement of the Tabernacle with its courts and furnishings. This time, let's go in as men already redeemed, searching for the deeper secret of consecration. Let us pause at each "throne of judgment" (Ps. 122:5), applying every point in the house to a spiritual aspect of our lives, personally and corporately. Judgment, order, and spiritual alignment must begin with us; otherwise there is no hope of restraining the wrath of God against the world (1 Pet. 4:17).

Since the building is not so important as the house within, and since we are searching for simple constant truth and practical application, perhaps we should, for our study of the house, go "back" to the original pattern given by God to

Moses in that old "Tabernacle," which David thought to "upgrade" to his personal standard of living! Here in the "text," as well as in Solomon's house, we will search for truth's application.

We are approaching the gate and we will proceed point by point through a simple Christian practicum in hope that while we have already glimpsed the blood and are redeemed, we may, within the veil, glimpse His glory and be transformed.

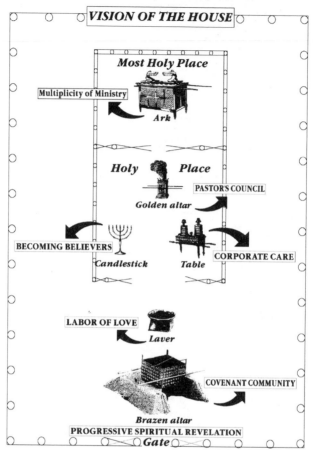

**VISION OF THE HOUSE**

**Most Holy Place**

Multiplicity of Ministry

*Ark*

**Holy Place**

PASTORS COUNCIL

*Golden altar*

BECOMING BELIEVERS

CORPORATE CARE

*Candlestick*    *Table*

LABOR OF LOVE

*Laver*

COVENANT COMMUNITY

*Brazen altar*

PROGRESSIVE SPIRITUAL REVELATION

*Gate*

The tabernacle the Lord described to Moses had three major sections or compartments: the outer court, the inner court or Holy Place, and the sanctuary or Most Holy Place. This is one of the most significant "threes" to appear in God's Word. The outer court was where sacrifices were offered to God for the sins of the people. Priest and non-priest alike were allowed in this area, along with the sacrifices they brought to the Lord.

Each court or section had furniture designed for specific functions, and made of specific materials. The first court contained the brazen altar and the brazen laver. In contrast, the second court contained a mixture of gold and wood articles, and those in the third court—the Most Holy Place—were made of pure gold.

# Chapter 6

# *The Gate of the House "Progressive Spiritual Concepts"*

*And thou shalt make the court of the tabernacle: for the south side southward there shall be hangings for the court of fine twined linen of an hundred cubits long for one side:*

*And the twenty pillars thereof and their twenty sockets shall be of brass; the hooks of the pillars and their fillets shall be of silver.*

*And for the gate of the court shall be an hanging of twenty cubits, of blue, and purple, and scarlet, and fine twined linen, wrought with needlework: and their pillars shall be four, and their sockets four.*

Exodus 27:9-10,16

It is impractical to look for answers and secrets concerning the gate without some information about the court. The court was an oblong rectangle that was twice as long as it was wide. It measured 100 cubits in length and 50 cubits in width, or about 175 feet long by 87½ wide. The height of the court curtain was a little more than 8½ feet.

The court structure was held up and bordered by 60 pillars set into brass sockets. These sockets could be buried in the sand and used as a foundation. Each pillar had a chapiter, or top piece, which was overlaid with silver and fitted with a silver hook for hanging the curtain. The pillars supported nearly 500 feet of fine linen curtains.

Thirty-five feet of blue, purple, scarlet, and fine linen suspended in the middle of the eastern side of the court formed the gate of the tabernacle. These brightly colored curtains hung over four of the pillars and marked the only entrance into the tabernacle.

---

We do not just lunge into a greater
dimension. There is a manner and
attitude of approach.

---

The court created a barrier and a pronounced manner of approach. The people in the camp outside the tent could not surge into or onto the tabernacle area—they had to follow a distinct avenue for entering. Following the redemption pattern of the tabernacle, Christ is the Door to the sheepfold. Jesus made it very clear that anyone "climbing up" or coming into the fold any other way was a thief and a robber (Jn. 10:1).

The examples go on and on. In fact, Moses' tabernacle, majestically crystalized in Solomon's temple, is a masterpiece of Bible typology, and it serves as the "Grandfather Clause" of all applied revelation. Although entire chapters could be written about the meaning of the courts, gates, foundation, etc., my mission is to show a present applied truth concerning the progressive revelation of God. The gate of the house clearly speaks of *more* than just entering into a structure of a building, but rather of entering into a position and alignment through which we may advance on into the deeper things of God.

Our approach to the gate requires a certain commitment. Although the gate is colorful and inviting, we must understand that *by moving through this opening we make ourself available and positioned for altars, sacrifices, and dyings.* There is a certain romance about revelation. Everybody wants to see more deeply into the things of God, but few are willing or ready to pay the price to "know Him" in the dimension Paul described, in "the power of His resurrection, and the fellowship of His sufferings" (Phil. 3:10)! We must have desire—an unquenchable thirst for Him, the true Temple—or we will never enter in.

Another important aspect of progressive spiritual revelation is the power and importance of God-ordained change. Change is elemental to the ongoing process of life, and especially to our life in the Spirit. However, change just for the sake of change is often dangerous, if not deadly.

True, divine alteration is a natural response to God's revelation and our spiritual discernment of His will. I must know what to change and what to leave in place. The process of advancement and spiritual adjustment requires that we understand the variables and constants in the Kingdom of God.

Some things must never change! For example, there will never be a substitute for the blood of Christ: "Neither is there salvation in any other: for there is none other name under heaven given among men, whereby we must be saved" (Acts 4:12). He will never leave us or forsake us

(Heb. 13:5). There are many other things that are eternally constant as well. They are as polar as the North Star; you can set your compass by them. They are true today and they will be true tomorrow. These are the "in Him" things! "In Him" there is no variableness, neither shadow of turning (Jas. 1:17). Such things as God's character, nature, and ability never change.

On the other hand, there are variables that certainly can change and many that should change—Do you have one or two services on Sunday? Do you wear a tie on Wednesday night? Are we obligated to have a new Sunday school wing, or do we even have to meet in a church building for that matter? What if we gathered in a corporate meeting only once a month?

The point I'm making is this: The constants must not change, but the variables can be expected to change. If I get my constants and variables mixed up, I'll miss the progressive revelation of God. What if He moves and I can't?! If I make my constants variables, I've created heresy by saying the unchanging God has changed. If I make my variables constant, I've created deadly tradition by enshrining the temporary in a place reserved for the eternal.

---

The traditions of men are the building blocks for spiritual idolatry.

---

Mary, the mother of Jesus, was a variable. *God could have chosen someone else*, but He chose her. She is the only woman in human history about whom the angel of the Lord said, "Blessed art thou among women" (Lk. 1:28). The leaders of the Roman Catholic Church made her a constant—a co-redeemer with Jesus—and created a doctrine that is believed by a large segment of the Christian world, despite the clear testimony of Scripture in Acts 4:12 and John 14:6.

Joseph, on the other hand, determined to "divorce himself" from the outrageous progressive concept that God had desired, and he suddenly found himself face to face with the angel of the Lord, who told him, "Don't be afraid to embrace the new and unusual—this is a holy thing!" (my paraphrase of Mt. 1:20).

Since the first trespass in the garden of Eden, we have continuously created man-made temples with broad religious gates, while the road or door to the house that God built is narrow and rarely entered.

First of all, no one can really approach the Kingdom or spiritual house of God unless the Spirit draws him... "Blessed is the man whom Thou choosest, and causest to approach unto Thee, that he may dwell in Thy courts: we shall be satisfied with the goodness of Thy house, even of Thy holy temple" (Ps. 65:4). The Holy Spirit must lead me through the maze of men's ideas into the pure river of God's revealed purpose. *I must be wooed by spiritual desire and not by worldly wantonness.* If I am motivated by desires for bigger churches, more income, greater ministerial recognition, or a multitude of other earthly reasons, I'll only see the grandeur of Solomon's temple of stone. The hidden manna, the secret key to David's spiritual house, lies buried within my own heart and *cannot be found short of absolute surrender and agonizing desire.*

The prophet Isaiah said, "For Zion's sake will I not hold My peace, and for Jerusalem's sake I will not rest, until the righteousness thereof go forth as brightness, and the salvation thereof as a lamp that burneth" (Is. 62:1). This fiery prophet was describing the effects of *divine discontentment.* God has sparked a fire in the hearts of His people that won't relent, it won't let up, it moves and propels us higher. In the heat of this holy unrest, each of us must declare: *I will not cease or stop my pursuit of the progressive revelation until God turns on all the lights and reveals the fullness of His purpose.* We must always be crying out to our God, "We want *more of You!*"

We should thank God for our yesterdays because we can't grow without them. They were our instructors and our counselors for a season, but although the character and nature of God never changes, His works, operations, and assignments to men on the earth do change. And the progress of His children is—by definition—*the process of change, metamorphosis, and constant conformation to the image of His Son.*

God is constantly adjusting the manner in which He deals with our approach to Him. There is no finding Him out! He is always becoming new to our earthly eyes as He reveals new aspects of the fullness of His purpose. Past blessings are appreciated, and old anointings become the substance of my thanksgiving, but I want to see what God is doing *now!* If the gate of the house becomes my entry into the great progressive spiritual concepts dear to God's heart, then I must catch a vision of the unseen and a glimpse into the invisible. *Anyone can casually view the obvious.* This is why we have countless volumes of religion pointing out, with over-used phrases and stale clichés, the need to hold on to our prized doctrinal and spiritual positions. We have measured and weighed the value of Solomon's house of stone, but few of us have dared to walk through the gate into the spiritual house that God built for David.

Jacob first encountered the unseen kingdom under the open sky, and it changed his life—and name—forever. On his first night away from home as he fled the wrath of his brother, Esau, Jacob left Beersheba and headed toward his uncle's home in Haran. In Genesis 28:11, it says that Jacob "lighted upon a certain place." That sounds to me like Jacob sort of "landed" there. In other words, he didn't make a reservation, there was no planned accommodation. This is simply where Jacob stopped!

The sandy ground became his pallet and stones were his pillow. Before the night was over, this place where Jacob "lighted" took on a whole new meaning! After visions of ladders, angels, and even the Lord God, Jacob boldly announced that the dry valley and rocky hillside of "Luz" was in fact the "*house of God...the gate of heaven*" (verse 17).

There was nothing to marvel about here, there was no evidence or archaelogical wonder to see—the rocks were not shaped like pillars, nor were the hills shaped like rectangular stones or altars. Jacob literally encountered the true temple of the Almighty; the house that God built was there in glorious spiritual visitation, and its gate revealed God's heavenly hosts ascending and descending, suspended between the celestial and the terrestrial!

Somewhere amid the dry stones of religion and the shallow pools of modern spirituality stands the Door—the living Gate to Heaven. Somewhere beyond the visible is the real temple!

I must be transformed—lifted to a higher dimension, focused on a greater vision. I'll never see the deeper things if I stay entangled in the casual mode of complacent Christianity. I must "press in," for as Jesus said, "the violent take it [the Kingdom] by force" (Phil. 3:14; Mt. 11:12).

I'll never truly enter into my ministry of Kingdom work until I get a holy hunger to throw down my cherished "old wineskin" and take on a deeper vessel of fullness of purpose and practice (Lk. 5:37-38).

The glaring parade of showy flesh marching through our pulpits and platforms must stop! We've heard enough glamorized parroting of untested thoughts, borrowed rampantly by multitudes of unanointed preachers from a precious too few fountains. No wonder the gold and silver of the temple is so attractive. No wonder the size of congregations, the number of voices in our choirs, and the value of our new facilities are key points in our promotional success stories! (There's nothing else to talk about!)

It's little wonder that the same pampered souls shun the altars and fires inside the house. It is far more convenient to offer an overall appraisal of Solomon's temple from without than to enter and know the "secret of God's tabernacle" from within.

There is a price to be paid by anyone who enters in. Pastors, teachers, ministers, and workers must stop the easy art of stealing another's vision and "borrowing" another's anointing. These practices only produce the awful and artificial tones of sounding brass and tinkling cymbals (1 Cor. 13:1). These thieves of the holy seek shortcuts and avoid every sacrifice as they continue to fashion graven images of "success" from a multitude of hollow ideas—while true vision languishes on the doorsteps of our modern spiritual clinics. We need a powerful renewing, a new and holy resolve to step out of the average and join the remnant revivalists who will not be satisfied with yesterday's manna or last year's inspiration. The gate of God's house is addressed by holy desire. Come, let us go up to the house of the Lord!

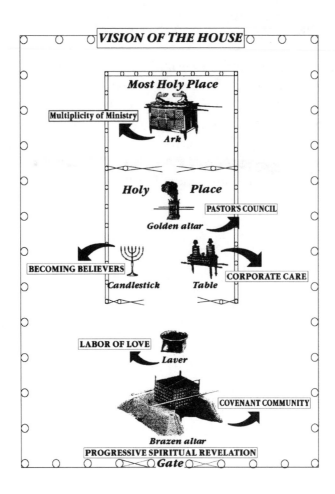

# VISION OF THE HOUSE

**Most Holy Place**

Multiplicity of Ministry

*Ark*

**Holy Place**

PASTOR'S COUNCIL

*Golden altar*

BECOMING BELIEVERS

*Candlestick*

*Table*

CORPORATE CARE

LABOR OF LOVE

*Laver*

COVENANT COMMUNITY

*Brazen altar*

PROGRESSIVE SPIRITUAL REVELATION

*Gate*

# Chapter 7

# *The Brazen Altar*
# *"Covenant Community"*

*And thou shalt make an altar of shittim [acacia] wood, five cubits long, and five cubits broad; the altar shall be foursquare: and the height thereof shall be three cubits.*

*And thou shalt make the horns of it upon the four corners thereof: his horns shall be of the same: and thou shalt overlay it with brass.*

*And thou shalt make his pans to receive his ashes, and his shovels, and his basons, and his fleshhooks, and his firepans: all the vessels thereof thou shalt make of brass.*

*And thou shalt make for it a grate of network of brass; and upon the net shalt thou make four brasen rings in the four corners thereof.*

*And thou shalt put it under the compass of the altar beneath, that the net may be even to the midst of the altar.*

*And thou shalt make staves for the altar, staves of shittim wood, and overlay them with brass.*

*And the staves shall be put into the rings, and the staves shall be upon the two sides of the altar, to bear it.*

> ***Hollow with boards shalt thou make it: as it was shewed thee in the mount, so shall they make it.***
>
> Exodus 27:1-8

Upon passing through the gate of the tabernacle of Moses, we are confronted by the largest of all the tabernacle (temple) furniture. This altar, built of shittim (or acacia) wood and overlaid with brass, was approximately seven feet square and more than five feet tall! It was here that the sacrifices were consumed. The holiness of God demanded that payment be made for sin before mercy could be offered. The offering had to be made by the offending person or by a substitute. It was at the altar that this offering was made to God.

## The Brazen Altar: There's One Sacrifice Left

It was to this brazen altar that the children of Israel brought their goats, bullocks, doves, and pigeons. This unending process could never take away sin; it only temporarily rolled the cloud of condemnation ahead year after year, waiting for that perfect "Lamb of God" who would once and for all take away the sin of the world!

We could go on with this redemption application and repeat what so many more able authors have expounded on for centuries—the altar's unavoidability, its absolute pertinence and application for personal repentance, the altar's finished work, and more.

The brazen altar is a landmark of redemption. It is an unmistakable type and shadow of the "foot of the cross," the nailing of the feet on the altar in Calvary's overview of the temple's layout. It is that first *"bleeding spot"* among a number of the sacrificial implements and articles. It certainly becomes the description in the Book of Revelation of the feet of the holy Christ, standing in the light (candlesticks) of the heavenly tabernacle with "feet like unto fine brass, as if they burned in a furnace" (Rev. 1:15).

Remember that we are using Moses' description of the furniture rather than Solomon's. By comparison to the seven-foot-square altar of Moses, Solomon built an altar measuring more than 30 feet square and 15 feet high (2 Chron. 4:1). On the day the temple was dedicated, Solomon offered 22,000 oxen and 120,000 sheep on this altar (2 Chron. 7:5). Obviously, the house and the foundation as well as the sacrifices were increased in beauty and volume.

We are, you will remember, looking for a house within this house—a meaning beyond the obvious meaning. Where is the house within this house of the desert? What is the meaning beyond the obvious meaning? The Hebrew word for "altar" is *mizbeach* (miz-bay'-akh), meaning to be the "slaughter place," the place of the shedding of the blood. Perhaps I'm just too practical, but since "Jesus paid it all" redemptively for us, that only leaves one sacrifice to be offered upon that brazen altar as we enter the "House That God Built."

I think the apostle Paul had found this "sacrifice that remains" when he confessed, "I am crucified with Christ: nevertheless I live; yet not I, but Christ liveth in me: and the life which I now live in the flesh I live by the faith of the Son of God, who loved me, and gave Himself for me" (Gal. 2:20). His message does not stop here. In fact, the next statement Paul makes is one of the most interesting in all of the New Testament—"I do not frustrate the grace of God...."

In my opinion, here lies the simplest and most profound truth of the temple plan. My paraphrase of what Paul is saying to the Galatian church is, "I refuse to get caught up in the multitude of applications and homiletical explanations of the Law and its paraphernalia—when Christ died, there is only one simple application left. I become the next sacrifice. Not one for sin; that's all paid. This one is for life and Kingdom purpose. *This is the sacrifice made upon entering into the "House That God Built."*

> *I beseech you therefore, brethren* [not sinners], *by the mercies of God* [not judgment], *that ye present your bodies a living sacrifice, holy, acceptable unto God, which is your reasonable service.*
>
> *And be not conformed to this world: but be ye transformed by the renewing of your mind, that ye may prove what is that good, and acceptable, and perfect, will of God.*

Romans 12:1-2

Paul believed in repeating his most important points over and over again. He doesn't stop with two sentences on the subject, he goes on:

> *For I say, through the grace* [there it is again] *given unto me, to every man that is among you, not to think of himself more highly than he ought to think; but to think soberly, according as God hath dealt to every man the measure of faith.*
>
> *For as we have many members in one body, and all members have not the same office:*
>
> *So we, being many, are one body in Christ, and every one members one of another.*

Romans 12:3-5

Paul had laid a foundation of truth in the first verse, and he spent the rest of the chapter driving home his vital points for the Body of Christ. He gives direct, specific instructions about community life and relationships in Christ's Body. He writes about "love without dissimulation...[being] kindly affectioned one to another with brotherly love...preferring one another...[being] fervent in spirit...rejoicing in hope; patient in tribulation; continuing instant in prayer; distributing to the necessity of saints; given to hospitality" (verses 9-13). Paul's appeal and description of Christian living offers us a true picture of abundant life in the greater house that God built.

Why is the brazen altar directly within the gate, squarely blocking all further progress? It forces us to embrace the true meaning of substitutionary sacrifice and personal responsibility under the atoning blood.

While others spend years explaining the importance and meaning of shittim wood, brass, staves, rings, pans, shovels, basins, and fleshhooks, Paul transcended the type in a spiritual application *that put himself on the altar* and nailed himself to Christ's cross! (And he did it while he was living, not after his death!)

When he says, "I do not frustrate the grace of God" (Gal. 2:21), he is simply saying, "If I'm going to see God's purpose and meaning, I must have a *renewed mind*—something in me must *change*!"

Fire is the great equalizer. It changes matter into gaseous substances—the heat of fire pushes the smoke upward. It burns up the dross—the chaff—and leaves the real substance. Hot fire produces pure gold! Paul's New Covenant application of Old Covenant type is more than instructional illustration—*it is the ultimate product of fiery baptism*. He says in essence, "If you are willing to die on that altar after having passed through the gate of the house with great desire, then you will lose your personal high mindedness—you become something that God can accept and use!"

The fire purges any ungodly attitude and consumes selfishness. Consequently, other people become important. They become one with you. We are left with honor, love, and patience for all the saints. In fact, we really become consumed into the *koinonia*—the fellowship of the brethren.

This is a far cry from the systemized religion that is flaunted so carelessly today. Religion haughtily hides hearts with no compassion, it metes out judgment and manifests the lukewarm spirit of the Laodiceans—who were "neither cold nor hot." Religion claims riches and increased good, while being wretched, miserable, poor, blind, and naked (Rev. 3:14-17). *The Savior's remedy* for this kind of unanointed crisis is to buy "gold tried in the fire" (Rev. 3:18).

There it is! The altar and its consuming fire confronts us and demands that we rise up before we can pass. We will never be a fellowship of believers without becoming a *covenant community.* The Word of God shows a pattern of establishing covenants by sacrifice. One of the first and most noted of the covenants was God's covenant with Abraham concerning the land. The Scriptures say that Abraham asked the Lord, "...whereby shall I know that I shall inherit it?" (Gen. 15:8) The later verses speak of an altar with five (5) major sacrifices, and the 17th verse states, "...when the sun went down, and it was dark, behold a smoking furnace, and a burning lamp that passed between those pieces. In the same day the Lord made a covenant with Abram..." (Gen. 15:17).

The gathering together of a remnant people will never come to pass if we continue to lean on our pitiful man-ordered, carnally operated religious organizations. As long as we continue to assemble groups of heady, high-minded, self-pleasing, jealously motivated, status-seeking preachers and people, we will only reproduce ourselves. Men whose eyes behold other men can only continue to produce a bastard religion in the earth, untried by fire and completely out of order before God! The altar awaits us and our works. We must ascend—it is a "must" if we are to manifest Christ in the earth!

David talked about the gathering of saints in Psalm 50:4-5, "The mighty God, even the Lord, hath spoken and called the earth the rising of the sun and the going down thereof. Out of Zion, the perfection of beauty, God hath shined. Our God shall come and shall not keep silence; a *fire* shall devour before Him and it shall be very tempestuous round about Him. He [God] shall call to the heavens from above, and to the earth, that He may judge His people [not sinners]. Gather My saints together unto Me; those that have made a covenant with Me by *sacrifice*."

It is obvious that there is no end to this subject, however, before I close this chapter, I'd like to make a few brief applications. God intends for our churches to be communities of people living, working, and loving together. From the Scriptures, we get the feeling that this community ("com"-with) or communion of the people is to love, guard, and give to each other.

Does it trouble you that members of our congregations are often so spoiled that they refuse to participate with other members they don't like? Are you disturbed when insignificant issues like church service times or the length of meetings become major issues of hot debate, while needy saints in the church are forgotten?

Is God's house really disrupted when the receiving of tithes and offerings is bypassed because the Holy Spirit sovereignly moves or brings conviction? Why is our rigid little religious system so disrupted when God steps into our midst and breaks the religious patterns of traditional gatherings and givings? I'm embarrassed to think of churches that would start to fall apart! These man-centered churches think God is small enough to contain in their religious system, and that He's too small to feed and provide for the holy thing that He births!

---

"Life style Christianity" is the only solution to carnal religion.

---

What would we do if our properties were taxed, if our precious facilities were seized, or if our religious freedom of assembly were revoked? What kind of house would we really have? Is there a "house of covenant" within our house? Is there a living, supernatural community in our "Church," a holy family bonded and molded together by a fiery covenant that cannot be shaken, no matter what we gain or lose?

If the gold, silver, and precious stones in our "Solomon's temple" is removed, will we really find a spiritual church—a body "built on the rock" by Christ, who alone is its builder?

We must pay the price to create a true fellowship through relationship. Just as carpenters endure uncounted smashed thumbs, cuts, splinters, and bruises to build even the finest of homes, so do Christians receive many wounds as they struggle to build covenant relationships among each other. Building relationships can be painful; so many of us choose to stick with older, unsanctified relationships, where the old life and the new mix uneasily. Whenever the fire of the altar burns us into more sincere and purposeful interactions, we may see some of the old friendships and liaisons disappear in the smoke of our holy cleansing.

There are costs to be met for deeper relationships with our husbands, wives, and children. Their social health is vital to their spiritual experience. We cannot ignore each other's needs and still claim to have a spiritual relationship to God. Finally, the church was divinely structured to "network," to function together as a living organism to foster health in the whole. God never intended for the pastor or his small staff to care for the whole body. That is a modern man-made custom born out of convenience, pride, and selfishness. Each of us must be "fitly joined together and compacted by that which every joint supplieth, according to the effectual working in the measure of every part, maketh increase of the body unto the edifying of itself in love" (Eph. 4:16). *Every part has a vital place and purpose in the house that God is building.*

Perhaps if we tie ourselves to the horns of the altar a little longer (*living sacrifices* have a way of crawling off!) we could reveal to the earth a Kingdom that cannot be taken away. The altar is one of the labors of the First Dimension (outer court). If we can't see the importance of the altar of sacrifice in our lives, then we may never see light in the Second Dimension (the sanctuary or Holy Place), and we may never behold the glory of the Third Dimension (Holy of Holies).

"Consecrate me now to Thy service, Lord, by the power of grace divine. Let my soul look up with a steadfast hope, and may my will be lost in Thine. Draw me nearer, blessed Lord!"

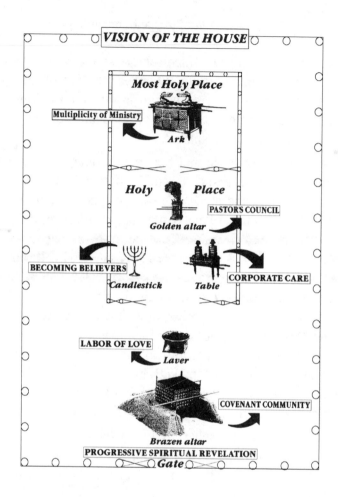

# VISION OF THE HOUSE

**Most Holy Place**

Multiplicity of Ministry

*Ark*

**Holy    Place**

PASTOR'S COUNCIL

*Golden altar*

BECOMING BELIEVERS

*Candlestick*    *Table*

CORPORATE CARE

LABOR OF LOVE

*Laver*

COVENANT COMMUNITY

*Brazen altar*

PROGRESSIVE SPIRITUAL REVELATION

*Gate*

# Chapter 8

# *The Brazen Laver*
## *"A Labor of Love"*

*And the Lord spake unto Moses, saying,*

*Thou shalt also make a laver of brass, and his foot also of brass, to wash withal: and thou shalt put it between the tabernacle of the congregation and the altar, and thou shalt put water therein.*

*For Aaron and his sons shall wash their hands and their feet thereat:*

*When they go into the tabernacle of the congregation, they shall wash with water, that they die not; or when they come near to the altar to minister, to burn offering made by fire unto the Lord:*

*So they shall wash their hands and their feet, that they die not: and it shall be a statute for ever to them, even to him and to his seed throughout their generations.*

Exodus 30:17-21

*And he made the laver of brass, and the foot of it of brass, of the lookingglasses of the women assembling [serving], which assembled [served] at the door of the tabernacle of the congregation.*

Exodus 38:8

Somehow the basic instructions God gave Moses for the construction of the tabernacle furniture seem simpler, less ornamental, than the expanded plans Solomon used. The laver is the least described of all the furniture of the tabernacle—it seems to be shrouded in mystery. The passages in Exodus give us no exact shape or size for the laver, nor are we told how this piece was to be transported when the tent was moved.

Solomon transformed the simple wash basin of the tabernacle into a "molten sea of ten cubits [15 feet across] from brim to brim" for the temple in Jerusalem (2 Chron. 4:2). The laver was 5 cubits (7½ feet) high, and the circumference of the huge pool measured 30 cubits (45 feet) around. The whole thing rested on the backs of four rows of 3 oxen, with all 12 cast in brass! The brass walls of the entire bowl were more than three inches thick, and its rim was decorated with fine filigree artwork of lilies. The laver held approximately 3,000 baths (25,500 gallons!). "He [Solomon] made also ten lavers, and put five on the right hand, and five on the left, to wash in them: such things as they offered for the burnt offering they washed in them; but the sea was for the priests to wash in" (2 Chron. 4:6).

What a contrast! Moses built a laver of unnamed proportion, while Solomon multiplied the laver's importance and prominence. I wonder what the real meaning is in the house that God built for David?

We do know that the laver Moses built was made from the "looking glasses" or polished brass mirrors of the women of Israel who gathered to serve and wait in anticipation at the entrance of the tabernacle. The brass mirrors they gave as freewill offerings for the work of the tabernacle represented a great sacrifice on their part. They must have been essential to their being well-kept and personally presentable. These women sacrificially gave that which reflected their outward beauty to help fashion a device that would cleanse the priests, who in turn offered sacrifices to cleanse the inward parts of their nation. They surrendered their reflective devices to make a reflecting pool for the priests to wash and prepare for service in the deeper "places" of the tabernacle.

Without question, their sacrifice was deeply spiritual. Peter wrote, "Whose adorning, let it not be that outward adorning of plaiting [braiding] the hair, and of wearing of gold, or of putting on of apparel; but let it be the hidden man of the heart, in that which is not corruptible, even the ornament of a meek and quiet spirit, which is in the sight of God of great price" (1 Pet. 3:3-4). In other words, we are not merely what we appear to be on the outside—there must be *hidden treasure* beyond the obvious.

The laver had a very specific purpose and use. It stood between the altar and the door of the holy place, and *it required a visit by every passing priest.* While the altar represented the purging by blood (Heb. 9:21-22), the laver represented priestly holiness and separation from the unclean, a cleansing of body as well as spirit.

Upon entering the priesthood, each priest washed "withal" at the laver; in other words, he washed all over. This certainly sounds like baptism, an act that follows the cleansing by blood. Once a priest had performed that first ceremony of cleansing and anointing for the whole body, the priest had only to wash his hands and feet when he entered the holy place of the tabernacle (the deeper things of God).

*For Aaron and his sons shall wash their hands and their feet thereat:*

*When they go into the tabernacle of the congregation, they shall wash with water, that they die not; or when they came near to the altar to minister, to burn offering made by fire unto the Lord:*

*So they shall wash their hands and their feet, that they die not....*

Exodus 30:19-21

God's Word is filled with "cleansing" passages. For example, Paul said we are sanctified and cleansed "with the washing of water by the Word" (Eph. 5:26). Jesus told His followers, "Now ye are clean through the word which I have spoken unto you" (Jn. 15:3). But none so touches me, or is so directly applicable to this subject as the words Jesus said to Peter, after he refused to allow Jesus to wash his feet, thinking it was below his Master's dignity.

*He [Jesus] riseth from supper, and laid aside His garments; and took a towel and girded Himself.*

*After that He poureth water into a bason [laver], and began to wash the disciples' feet, and to wipe them with the towel wherewith He was girded.*

*Then cometh He to Simon Peter: and Peter saith unto Him, Lord, dost Thou wash my feet?*

*Jesus answered and said unto him, What I do thou knowest not now; but thou shalt know hereafter.*

John 13:4-7

Jesus seems to be revealing to Peter and His other disciples one of the Kingdom secrets—one of the keys, perhaps, to David's house. Is it possible that we have here the *key to the laver*?

"Peter saith unto Him, Thou shalt never wash my feet. Jesus answered him, If I wash thee not, thou hast no part with Me" (verse 8). In essence, Jesus was saying, "If you don't go through this process with Me, you have no part with Me!" Was Jesus speaking of the shedding of blood and remission of sin? No, I don't believe so. The following passage tells us exactly what process Jesus had in mind. It had to do altogether with serving one another...*the labor of love*!

Notice how Simon Peter responds once he understands the Lord's meaning—"Lord, not my feet only, but also my hands and my head" (verse 9). Peter threw himself over the pattern and said, *"Wash me at the laver of love and servanthood so I can go on up into Your fullness...from the altar of sacrifice at the foot of the cross to the ark of the covenant crowning Your headship."*

Notice that the laver is placed above the foot of the cross *at the next bleeding spot.* It was from Jesus' side that blood and *water* flowed! Here was the pouring out—it is here at the laver, above the foot of the altar of sacrifice, that we find water of cleansing! Jesus continued, "He that is washed [loved, baptized, redeemed] needeth not save to wash his feet, but is clean every whit..." (Jn. 13:10a). After refering to Judas in the second part of this verse, stating that Judas was not involved in the cleansing, Jesus asked the others, "Know ye what I have done to you?" (Jn. 13:12b)

Here comes the most powerful truth of the whole episode! "If I then, your Lord and Master, have washed your feet; *ye also ought to wash one another's feet.* For I have given you an example, that ye should do as I have done to you. Verily, verily [the double imperitive of Deity which means *pay attention!*], I say unto you, The SERVANT is not greater than his lord..." (Jn. 13:14-16).

There it is: The entire matter of the washing and cleansing of the laver has to do, not with what is done for us, but with what we do for each other! Here in the true house is the revelation of the heart of a servant—the *Labor of Love*. No matter how much blood has been shed and sacrifice made for us, we will not progress into the house that God built without the true spirit of Christ who gave Himself for others.

It is impossible to wash another person's feet without washing your hands! So the spiritual cleansing by the Spirit is born out of loving interaction and care for each other. Jesus invited His terrified disciples to renew their fellowship with Him by saying, "Behold My hands and My feet, that it is I Myself" (Lk. 24:39a). One of the qualifications for true Christian widowhood, according to First Timothy 5:10, was that she had washed the feet of the saints. The ceremony of literal feet washing is valuable for us today, but what we have here goes far beyond the physical practice.

Labor appears prominently in the New Testament. The Lord knew the labor and patience of the Ephesian church (Rev. 2:2). The apostle Paul wrote to the church at Corinth, "your labor is not in vain in the Lord" (1 Cor. 15:58). In Second Corinthians 5:9, he said, in essence, that we labor to be acceptable to God (once we belong to His family). Hebrews 6:10a says God "is not unrighteous to forget your work and labor of love." Paul remembered the labor of love bestowed upon him by the church at Thessalonica (1 Thess. 1:3). And in the Book of Hebrews, 4:11, the writer says, "Let us labor...to enter into that rest."

Our labor must not be works for salvation, but rather the attitude of serving each other in our passage into the rest—the deeper places in God! We must forget ourselves (give up our mirrors) as we behold the needs of others.

As we look into the perfect law of liberty and continue in it, James writes that if we remember God's Word and *do the work* (labor), "this man shall be blessed in his deed" (Jas. 1:25). The twenty-seventh verse goes on to say that "pure [washed] religion and undefiled before God and the Father is this, To visit the fatherless and widows in their affliction, and to keep himself unspotted from the world."

There is a bonding in nature that begins and grows through touch. The fallow deer, for example, licks the newborn fawn until it can get on its feet! A mother clinches an unspoken bond with her baby through the months of gestation.

Relationships are created and strengthened by words and touch. Mature relationships allow deeper interaction, but the church often has no bonding process for its members. The people just go to the same building and say the same religious phrases. Where is the bonding; where is the helping hand—the manifestation of unconditional love?

How many of the hands lifted in praise to God in our sanctuaries are "unholy hands" (1 Tim. 2:8), because they have not washed the feet of a brother or sister in a labor of love? Too often we search for depth in God while bypassing the laver.

Three "T's" or crosses are attached to the laver. Each "T" represents something we possess *that must be shared* with the Kingdom as family members in the house that God is building.

The first "T" is Time. We are so busy doing worldly and earthly things that it's often difficult to find anyone associated with the church who has time for anything.

The next "T" represents Talent. We all have gifts and abilities that the Kingdom could use. Once we discover our talent and are willing to release it to the Church, we need patience to learn where our gifting "fits."

The next "T" is Treasure. For our own spiritual health, we must give our money—tithes and offerings given out of willing and cheerful hearts. Keep in mind that Jesus said, "For where your treasure is, there will your heart be also" (Mt. 6:21). Our hearts must be on the altar, not in our pocketbooks.

This is no new story; however, I think a small application here could enhance the "laver labor of love."

Perhaps our churches should make available to each of its members a comprehensive list of needs in the Kingdom family—everything from paint to pistons, from floors to flowers. If each covenant member agreed to give some of those "T's" (their time, talent, or treasure) in certain areas when called upon, those needs would rapidly disappear.

Modern computers allow instant matching of needs to "T's," so carpenters could be found with the touch of a button, and hostesses gathered with a simple call. What if Christianity become a *"Christ art"* again, where we master the spiritual art of being like Christ. How can we best hook up with God's Spirit to pick up one another's burdens, to set each other and the Kingdom free?

When God's earthly Body functions as it was designed to *work*, the financial expenditures for working staff members and hired labor could be instantly reduced by the labor of love from the whole Body. The tithes and offerings could be used to assemble a stronger armada of *pure* Word ministry, speaking into the life of the Church. Other precious funds could be channeled to care for the needy and reach the lost.

Does this sound idealistic? Not at all! We' just have to *give up our mirrors.*

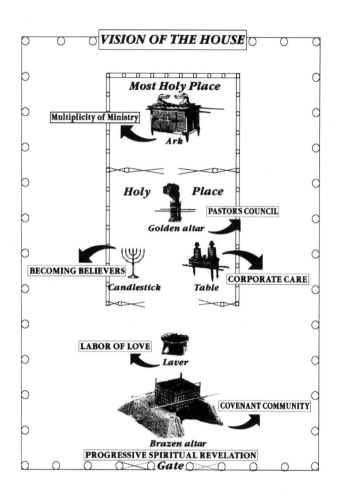

# VISION OF THE HOUSE

**Most Holy Place**

**Multiplicity of Ministry**

*Ark*

**Holy Place**

**PASTOR'S COUNCIL**

*Golden altar*

**BECOMING BELIEVERS**

*Candlestick*

*Table*

**CORPORATE CARE**

**LABOR OF LOVE**

*Laver*

**COVENANT COMMUNITY**

*Brazen altar*

**PROGRESSIVE SPIRITUAL REVELATION**

*Gate*

# Chapter 9

# *The Golden Candlestick*
# *"Becoming Believers"*

*And thou shalt make a candlestick of pure gold: of beaten work shall the candlestick be made: his shaft, and his branches, his bowls, his knops, and his flowers, shall be of the same.*

*And six branches shall come out of the sides of it; three branches of the candlestick out of the one side, and three branches of the candlestick out of the other side:*

*Three bowls made like unto almonds, with a knop and a flower in one branch; and three bowls made like almonds in the other branch, with a knop and a flower: so in the six branches that come out of the candlestick.*

*And in the candlestick shall be four bowls made like unto almonds, with their knops and their flowers.*

*And there shall be a knop under two branches of the same, and a knop under two branches of the same, and a knop under two branches of the same, according to the six branches that proceed out of the candlestick.*

*Their knops and their branches shall be of the same: all it shall be one beaten work of pure gold.*

*And thou shalt make the seven lamps thereof: and they shall light the lamps thereof, that they may give light over against it.*

*And the tongs thereof, and the snuffdishes thereof, shall be of pure gold.*

*Of a talent of pure gold shall he make it, with all these vessels.*

*And look that thou make them after their pattern, which was showed thee in the mount.*

Exodus 25:31-40

We've passed through the First Dimension of the tabernacle which is the place of basic labor. Now we're entering the sanctuary, the Second Dimension with its increased value and purpose.

Everything in the First Dimension was fashioned with brass. Brass speaks of man's things. The furniture of the Second Dimension is overlaid with gold, a type of Deity, representing God and His purity. I should add, however, that the furniture of the sanctuary, while being overlaid with gold, still requires man's labor and participation. The lamps must be filled with oil, the shewbread must be baked and placed on the table, and the incense must be created and poured out upon the golden altar. So the Second Dimension is the realm of God-man participation. Here we are still "laboring to enter," we are still reaching for the holiest place of all.

The first piece of furniture to be studied in the sanctuary is the golden candlestick—we are drawn to it by its obvious light. The first impression I get when studying this ancient lampstand is the combination of its fundamental structure coupled with its extremely detailed ornamentation.

There are no light switches, no glowing bulbs or dimmers—this piece of furniture is fundamental in its creation. It is really a rack or stand holding seven oil lamps, or *candles* as they were called. The lamps evidently had wicks because we are told they were trimmed, and the wick's residue was emptied into snuffdishes.

Before we get to the golden structure of the stand itself, I am impressed by the amount of tedious care required to keep the lamps burning. This is a picture of practical diligence and patience. It is interesting to note that this type of light was maintained by "the consumption of substance," in this case, oil of the purest type. It had to be constantly and carefully replenished by the priests so that the light was never extinguished in the temple. The Lord required that the light burn on in an unbroken flame from generation to generation.

May I pause here to say that this golden candlestick and its care truly represent an unending, never-finished project? Add this to the fact that light in the Scriptures represents the unending function of learning, understanding, and revelation.

Now I have set the basis for designating this chapter on the golden candlestick, "Becoming Believers." I am convinced that the believer never *arrives* in his search for godly knowledge and understanding. Growing up into Christ is an enlightening experience. "God is light, and in Him is no darkness at all" (1 John 1:5). "That was the true Light, which lighteth every man that cometh into the world" (Jn. 1:9). Our passage into the deeper knowledge of Christ requires a never-ending search for light, involving diligence and much patience.

Our study of the golden candlestick parallels the work of God in the house He is building, as He helps us "become believers."

Jesus called His disciples and said, "Follow Me and I will make you to *become* fishers of men" (see Mk. 1:17). The key here is the process of "becoming" in God.

The average Christian wants to "be" something in the Kingdom and often is satisfied with having "arrived" at one point or another. But the call to the Holiest Place beyond the veil does not allow our *arrival*–it requires our constant involvement in the process of *becoming*.

This is the "faith-to-faith" activity. Here we go from victory to victory and from glory to glory (Rom. 1:17, 2 Cor. 3:18). The golden candlestick tells us that our quest for light and revelation must never be a destination. We must continually fuel the fire if we are to become like Him.

In this house that God is building, there are still some very basic principles to be understood; some foundational spiritual "character shapers" that are never out of date. According to our limited information, it is estimated that the golden candlestick weighed about 130 pounds, and it was made of solid, beaten gold. It had a main stem with three branches extending up on either side, and was the most ornate and beautiful of all the temple furniture, although it was not cast in a mold. Bezaleel, the anointed artificer who created this piece, literally beat it out of a block of solid gold.

This speaks to me of an unprecedented creation–something that only the Holy Spirit could accomplish through Bezaleel, the anointed man of God. Furthermore, it urges me to believe that the major criteria for receiving the vision and the revelation of God's true house is not so much a practiced art as it is *a pounding out* of direction through prayer, fasting, and diligent study of the Word of God. True godly vision evolves through a "becoming process."

Our seminaries and religious colleges continue to pump out carbon copies of failed ministries—all doctrinally shiny and homiletically correct, while *divine revelation* languishes in the pulpits and parishioners perish in the pews!

Our man-made religious lampstands appear to be sophisticated on the outside, but within they are hollow, and our traditional wicks are smoky. We've managed to produce cheap light and low power. Rarely can we find that bleeding heart that cries, *I am willing to "become" a believer, a minister, a living sacrifice—make me what I ought to be.*

As we have stated before, this lampstand consisted of a main stem or shaft, with three branches emerging upward on either side of the trunk. It would be easy to spend our time explaining that Christ is the vine (the main shaft) and we are the branches. We could go into a great deal of detail about the design of the bowls, the knobs, the flowers and other attending articles. However, we are searching for the meaning beyond our redemptive participation. What is the practical application of the candlestick in the Vision of the house that God is building on the earth today?

Consider with me the fact that the candlestick was in the sanctuary, the inner court, and its main purpose was to *give light while being enlightened.* I am satisfied that the light shown on the Bread (the *koinonia*), and highlighted the Altar of Incense (purposeful worship). It is also my conviction that the light in this dimension was not seen from the first court, and it was certainly not needed in the Most Holy Place! In other words, the light of the golden candlestick was concentrated in type and shadow on the local fellowship and its spiritual responsibility.

Let me become even more practical and say that I feel there are major areas of instruction necessary in every local setting, regardless of the main focus in that particular ministry. In order to have order, there are basic principles that must be taught. These basic principles create light and the understanding necessary for successful spiritual function; again, regardless of the local focus or vision in each setting. Remember the candlestick had three branches sweeping through the main stem on either side. These three branches represent three primary areas of spiritual development that are essential to the Vision of the House. Accepting the risk of being too simple or even abstract, I'm going to name these fundamental and basics areas of light.

The first branch is a type of "foundational doctrinal truth." Jesus called His disciples from their secular occupations and immediately began teaching them the things concerning the Kingdom of God (Mk. 4:11).

Every believer has the right to receive light concerning what has happened to him in his new birth and what is expected of him as a Christian. If he is going to grow, he must have a *good foundation*. A concentrated study of the "first principles" strengthens the "root system" so that when other light and revelation is applied, the tree won't be top-heavy and broken over.

In many of our more modern Charismatic circles, we have major emphasis placed on faith and the supernatural gifts and ministries, while the nurturing and admonition of the Lord to stand and become fitted into the Kingdom purpose is lost.

Sadly, many precious souls are encouraged and taught that there is no price to be paid for service. Therefore, they believe that the hammering out process of "becoming" a useful instrument is unnecessary and a useless waste of spiritual energy. Consequently, we see great numbers of disillusioned folks busily searching for a place to "go forth in their gift" or be "recognized in an Ascension gift ministry" who do not understand the simplest truths about the eternal purpose of God or the responsibilities of Christian priesthood and service.

Very often, these same unsettled souls make up a large band of nomadic Christians who are constantly shaking the dust off their feet in spiritual rejection and drifting on, looking for other places to disrupt, while they themselves are servants of ignorance and corruption. Without foundation, they claim that all authority is bondage, and fundamental instruction is legislation.

With all of the "streams" and "camps" in Christianity focusing on and majoring on their pet themes, there must be an increased effort to bring a wholeness to believers by offering *balance without compromise* and *foundations without bondage*. Otherwise, we will continue to sire multitudes of spiritually "genetically" deprived ministries who haven't the foggiest notion of the greater purposes of God and His house.

This brings me to the second branch of the candlestick, which I am going to call "spiritual authority." According to the Word of God, we must all be submitted to the "higher powers" (Rom. 13:1). Each of us has a definite need to be responsible to someone or to something.

Authority is the key to all security and peace. Without the guidance and security of authority, a child cannot learn from a teacher; a son cannot receive instruction from his father; and a citizen cannot rest peacefully at night. Without authority, it is impossible to drive an automobile, shop in a mall, or buy groceries at the store. Authority is the response system by which all government, whether good or evil, is maintained.

While basic doctrine teaches us our relationship to God, spiritual authority teaches our relationships and responsibilities to each other. If a son does not respect the authority of his father, he will soon be faced with authority from teachers. If he does not respect the authority of the teachers, he will soon be faced with the authority of the police. If he does not respect the authority of the police, he will be faced with the authority of the judge. If he does not respect the authority of the judge, he will be faced with the authority of the warden. If he does not respect the authority of the warden, he is faced with the authority of a lethal injection, the electric chair, or the gas chamber—there he meets the authority of God! What is true in the natural is also true in the spiritual. Somewhere in life—and hopefully early—we must learn to submit to authority.

If a young Christian does not learn to fear God and respect those who have the "rule over him," a course is often set which is similar to that of an undisciplined son. The longer the trail, the more pain and spiritual disruption they cause. The Bible says the end of those who do not submit is always death (see Rom. 6:21). The list is too long to set forth here, but among those who met this end are King Saul, Balaam, Korah, Achan, and Judas Iscariot.

In the house that God is building, no one should be placed in authority until they have first submitted to instruction in foundational doctrine and spiritual authority. Those who have never submitted and served must never rule. Rebellious souls who resist authority and misunderstand the value of submission and service become spiritual tyrants in the Church, warlords in their generation, and gang leaders on their streets. If one has not borne the whip, he cannot know the pain he inflicts by his scourging. Those who have not accepted correction can never offer mercy and compassion. Self-appointed "spiritual surgeons" who have not been wounded can never heal a bleeding heart. Perhaps we should learn again that "if we suffer [with Him], we shall also reign with Him" (2 Tim. 2:12a)!

After foundational doctrine and spiritual authority, we are ready to light the third branch of the candlestick. I call this one "Care Leadership Training." It is here that we learn how to care for the needs of the Body as we shine our light on the Bread.

Care leadership training is a diligent study in understanding the needs and responses of God's people at every level. Sometimes the needs of these people stem from ignorance or because they are totally "out of the way" (Heb. 12:13). Others are pressed with unusual circumstances ranging from financial needs to marriage problems. There is no end to constant needs arising out of a local congregation.

In our past history, the answer was, "We pay the preacher, let him handle it." But in the mature and growing house that God is building, the "pastor" is allowed the blessing of divine pursuits, while the strong accept the care of the weaker ones in the Body. As we learn to "bear ye one another's burdens," we are fulfilling the law of Christ (Gal. 6:2). This is where the light really shines—"By this shall all men know that ye are My disciples, if ye have love one to another" (Jn. 13:35). It is here, in the realm of godly deeds and true spirituality, that the *real house* is seen and the true Body of Christ comes to light.

Through understanding our relationship to God, our relationship to each other, and finally our relationship to the purpose, we become a true habitation of His Spirit and a positive representative of His grace. Here all selfishness is lost and personal praise is unimportant. The believer has become a golden vessel—hammered out through the painful process of submission and service until he cries out with the great apostle, *"I am crucified with Christ: nevertheless I live; yet not I, but Christ liveth in me"* (Gal. 2:20).

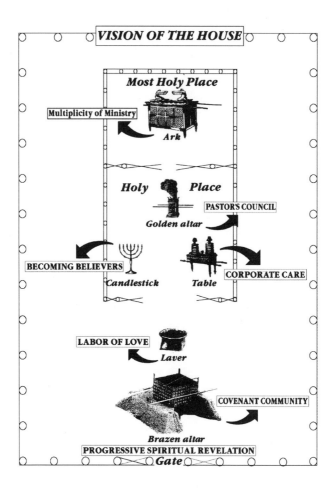

# VISION OF THE HOUSE

**Most Holy Place**

Multiplicity of Ministry

*Ark*

**Holy Place**

PASTOR'S COUNCIL

*Golden altar*

BECOMING BELIEVERS

*Candlestick*

*Table*

CORPORATE CARE

LABOR OF LOVE

*Laver*

COVENANT COMMUNITY

*Brazen altar*

PROGRESSIVE SPIRITUAL REVELATION

*Gate*

# Chapter 10

# *The Table of Shewbread*
# *"Corporate Care"*

*Thou shalt also make a table of shittim wood: two cubits shall be the length thereof, and a cubit the breadth thereof, and a cubit and a half the height thereof.*

*And thou shalt overlay it with pure gold, and make thereto a crown of gold round about...*

*And thou shalt make for it four rings of gold, and put the rings in the four corners that are on the four feet thereof...*

*And thou shalt set upon the table shewbread before Me alway.*

Exodus 25:23-30

*And the table and his furniture, and the pure candlestick with all his furniture, and the altar of incense.*

Exodus 31:8

*And he made the table of shittim wood: two cubits was the length thereof, and a cubit the breadth thereof, and a cubit and a half the height thereof:*

*And he overlaid it with pure gold, and made thereunto a crown of gold round about.*

*Also he made thereunto a border of an handbreadth round about; and made a crown of gold for the border thereof round about.*

*And he cast for it four rings of gold, and put the rings upon the four corners that were in the four feet thereof.*

*Over against the border were the rings, the places for the staves to bear the table.*

*And he made the staves of shittim wood, and overlaid them with gold, to bear the table.*

*And he made the vessels which were upon the table, his dishes, and his spoons, and his bowls, and his covers to cover withal, of pure gold.*

Exodus 37:10-16

*And thou shalt take fine flour, and bake twelve cakes thereof: two tenth deals shall be in one cake.*

*And thou shalt set them in two rows, six on a row, upon the pure table before the Lord.*

*And thou shalt put pure frankincense upon each row, that it may be on the bread for a memorial, even an offering made by fire unto the Lord.*

*Every sabbath he shall set it in order before the Lord continually, being taken from the children of Israel by an everlasting covenant.*

*And it shall be Aaron's and his sons'; and they shall eat it in the holy place: for it is most holy unto him of the offerings of the Lord made by fire by a perpetual statute.*

Leviticus 24:5-9

*For there was a tabernacle made; the first, wherein was the candlestick, and the table, and the shewbread; which is called the sanctuary.*

Hebrews 9:2

Across the room, against the north side of the sanctuary, stood the table of shewbread, illuminated and made visible in the never-ending light of the candlestick. This serving table, being three feet long, 1½ feet wide and 2¼ feet high, was made of shittim wood and overlaid with gold. The dual compounding of the materials, as I stated before, speaks of the God-man participation unique to the second dimension of the shadow type. The size of this table seems limited to its purpose, which means that it was used for nothing else, save the presentation and serving of the shewbread.

Again, volumes could be written concerning the application of spiritual things to this natural creation and its accompanying articles. We could devote paragraph after paragraph expanding on the heavenly meaning of the general size, height, and width of the table. Add the proposed meaning of the combination of materials, and then further meditate on the border, the two crowns, rings, staves, dishes, chargers, spoons, covers, bowls (sometimes interpreted "flagons" and "chalices").

This unending study of these pieces from the redemptive point of view brings us again and again to the conclusion that this table of shewbread is truly representative of the "Table of the Lord," the Communion table. Our feeling is further confirmed by the passage, "...in the holy place shalt thou cause the strong wine to be poured unto the Lord for a drink offering" (Num. 28:7). These offerings were obviously not poured on the golden altar as some suppose, but rather into those "flagons" and "chalices" accompanying this table of shewbread. Here then, certainly, we have *the bread and the wine.*

Now this redemptive revelation cries for even greater examination. But may I leave this precious pursuit to you and other more studied and eloquent scholars? I want to digress back in this chapter to a comparatively mundane and practical application of the whole shewbread issue.

In my digression to a simple practicum for the house, I must flow back through these wonderful texts: "God furnished a table in the wilderness" (Ps. 78:19). "Thou preparest a table in the presence of mine enemies" (Ps. 23:5). "Wisdom hath furnished her table" (Prov. 9:2). "Thou shalt be filled at my table" (Ezek. 39:20). "...Crumbs from the master's table" (Mt. 15:27). "You may eat and drink at my table" (Lk, 22:30). Finally, the Book of Hebrews 9:1-6, says, "Then verily the first covenant had also ordinances of divine service, and a worldly sanctuary. For there was a tabernacle made; the first, wherein was the candlestick, and the table, and the shewbread; which is called the sanctuary."

My digression leads me even further as I consider the shewbread. "I will satisfy the poor with bread" (Ps. 132:15). "His land shall be satisfied with bread" (Prov. 12:11). "He giveth his bread to the poor" (Prov. 22:9). "Eat thy bread with joy and drink" (Eccles. 9:7). "Cast thy bread upon the waters" (Eccles. 11:1). "...Land of bread and vineyards" (Is. 36:17). "Deal thy bread to the hungry" (Is. 58:8) "Give to us our daily bread" (Mt. 6:11). "He was known in the breaking of bread" (Lk. 24:35). "I am the Bread of Life" (Jn. 6:35). "Breaking bread from house to house" (Acts 2:46).

I am however, more than anything else, smitten by the number of loaves on the table—that number being 12. This, while considering all the other typical applications, speaks to me of the representative number of the tribes of Israel or the whole number of God's people. Coupled with the apostle Paul's New Testament Scripture, it confirms my deepest interest:

*Wherefore, my dearly beloved, flee from idolatry.*

*I speak as to wise men; judge ye what I say.*

*The cup of blessing which we bless, is it not the communion of the blood of Christ? The bread which we break, is it not the communion of the body of Christ?*

*For we being many are one bread, and one body: for we are all partakers of that one bread.*

1 Corinthians 10:14-17

This astonishing passage states that we, the believers, being the body of Christ in the earth, are literally that "one bread." As the twelve loaves represented the unity and wholeness of the bread, so the communion (*koinonia*) of the body of Christ is the "whole" or one bread, "...for we being many are one bread, and one body."

I am therefore concentrating my energies in this treatise to the varied aspects of the bread itself. In understanding the number, contents, texture, and process of the loaves with their creation and presentation, I may very well come into a revelation concerning the body of Christ, and more particularly, the house that God is building in the earth right now.

The word "table" in the Hebrew, *shulchan*, means "a meal, as spread out, to stretch forth and to sow." This table is a place of supply, a place of "spreading out" or offering care.

I must also be willing to stretch myself toward my brother and sister in Christ—I must be willing to be given for them.

No other piece of furniture in the tabernacle plan supplied any personal sustenance to the priests or servants of the Lord. This table alone, is the place of personal priestly provision. This one article represents the personal touch of care for the priestly need. Furthermore, the word "shewbread" in the Hebrew, *lecham*, means "to feed on; to consume, devour, eat," and consequently, "to battle, prevail and to overcome." We get the sense that when we care for each other, when we are willing to be consumed or used by each other, that we actually do battle and prevail over our common enemy.

Thus, I have named this shewbread chapter "Corporate Care." We are searching for the answer to locating, presenting, and maintaining the care and victory so desperately needed in the body.

The shewbread was created to be consumed by the priests. The Scripture clearly states that Aaron and his sons were to eat it (Lev. 24:9). The shewbread was also called "the most Holy offering made by fire." In other words, no greater sacrifice could be made than that which sustains the priesthood, the body! This sounds like Paul when he said, "...I will very gladly spend and be spent for you" (2 Cor. 12:15).

Our house also needs a rebaptism in understanding the words "no greater love [offering] hath a man than to lay down his life for his friends" (Jn. 15:13). At the table where the priest receives personal sustenance, there is a defined care, one for the other.

Jesus, in one of His most caring stories, stated that the good Samaritan told the host to "take care" of the beaten man (Lk. 10:35).

The apostle Paul, wrote to the Corinthians:

*That there should be no schism in the body* [bread]*; but that the members should have the* same care *one for another.*

*And whether one member suffer, all the members suffer with it; or one member be honored, all the members rejoice with it.*

*Now ye are the body of Christ, and members in particular.*

1 Corinthians 12:25-27

Now consider with me that we, being the body, the one bread, are also "...a *royal priesthood*...that ye should shew forth [shewbread] the praises of Him who hath called you out of darkness [outer court] into His marvelous light [the sanctuary with candlesticks]" (1 Pet. 2:9).

Here now begins the seemingly great paradox: How can the bread and the priests (all believers) be the same? Ah! No paradox here. We have become partakers of the divine nature (2 Pet. 1:4). We are now the sons of God. Through this transformation, we, like Christ, become both the sacrifice and the sacrificer (Heb. 9:11; 7:27). He was both the lamb destined for the altar, and the High Priest who willingly offered up Himself. We become the priest who eats the bread, and the bread that is consumed. In other words, we feed on and from each other.

Now let us try to pull all the ends together.

We being the body of Christ must be extended out to each other as the table. We also must allow that which is upon us or within us to be freely given and consumed by each other. We, through this process of giving and receiving care, set up a tremendous "battle line" against satan—through which we prevail and overcome (Hebrew, *lacham*).

We need each other. It is easy to say, "God will take care of us," but in reality *He cares through us!* The body of Christ is broken and wounded only because we have never learned the real kingdom truth of "freely giving and freely receiving" (Mt. 10:8), and that from one another. I am almost consumed with the Scripture, "Bear ye one another's burdens, and so fulfil ye the law of Christ" (Gal. 6:2).

Another aspect of the shewbread was that it was made with finely ground flour.

The difference between "flour" and "fine flour" is that the word, flour, stems from a word that means "to grind," whereas *fine flour* means "to strip." I find the texture of the shewbread a very unique and powerful type of the spiritual processes necessary for the average believer to become palatable for "care consumption." The breaking down by tribulation, the grinding of unusual situations, and finally, the stripping away of every carnal thing leaves no possible means of self-glorification.

Also, the process of grinding and stripping leaves no large or small grains—no individual identity—we are all truly one. The Book of Hebrews, chapter 5, verses 1-5, explains the grinding process order we go through to become a priestly participant.

After the firing or baking process, the bread is covered with pure frankincense. This substance is very flammable and quickly ignited. The Hebrew words for "pure frankincense" (*zakak-laban*) means "to be free-flowing and giving of its substance." Could we agree that the frankincense only aids in expressing the believer's willingness to be consumed without resistance or reluctance.

The shewbread, which I also call "the *koininia*," the Body of Christ, was to be set on the table before the Lord always. In other words, the whole body was to constantly be presented before the Lord. The epistle to the Ephesians says that all kinds of prayer and supplication in the Spirit should *always* be made (with carefulness) "for all [the whole body] saints" (Eph. 6:18). So our first practical effort in "caring for the bread" is so foundational that it is almost overlooked and often forsaken or forgotten. We must pray for each other! This must be first, because properly praying for each other is the key to sensing and understanding the needs of each other.

"Likewise the Spirit also helpeth our infirmities: for we know not what we should pray for as we ought: but the Spirit itself maketh intercession for us with groanings which cannot be uttered. And He that searcheth the hearts knoweth what is the mind of the Spirit, because He maketh intercession for the saints according to the will of God" (Rom. 8:26-27). Notice that the Spirit, through prayer, makes intercession for the saints and because of that, "...all things work together for good..." (Rom. 8:28).

What I see last in this type is depicted by the third branch of the candlesticks—"Care Leadership Training."

In our old outer court mentality, the peacher was the church slave, and the people exacted a high price from him in endless offerings of personal time and energies.

In this house that God is building, however, the body must grow in Kingdom consciousness: rather than one or two pastors or elders trying to care for the entire flock, the believers help shoulder the load and share a common care for each other.

From this spiritually increased mentality of consuming and being consumed, we experience the very important ministry of care through interpersonal relationships. The apostle Paul called this the "ministry of the saints" (1Cor. 16:15).

While the set ministry and eldership must certainly handle the major crises of a congregation and minister to the corporate gathering, the "care groups" (loaves of bread) should be organized to gather information, assist with emergencies, initiate external fellowship aimed toward better understanding of each others' needs and the forging of new relationships.

Corporate care is often thought to be just the ministry to the singly gathered body. I am, however, still thinking of the 12 loaves and also of the 12 baskets—remember those. They were the ones left over after Jesus had taken the lad's whole lunch and broke it into pieces. He then gave to His disciples and they gave to the multitude. Interesting, isn't it? Jesus takes the whole, breaks it and gives it. The result is the gathering of 12 times the amount of the initial offering. This is the fruit of the shewbread (*koinonia*), under the divine illumination of the candlestick in the House that God built.

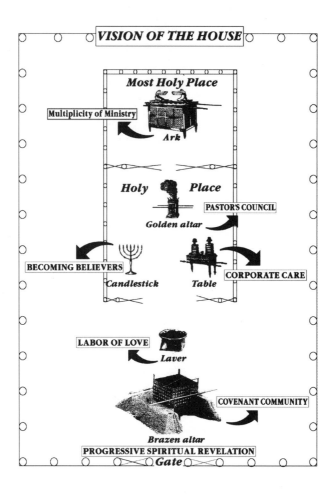

# VISION OF THE HOUSE

**Most Holy Place**

Multiplicity of Ministry

*Ark*

**Holy** **Place**

PASTORS COUNCIL

*Golden altar*

BECOMING BELIEVERS

CORPORATE CARE

*Candlestick*        *Table*

LABOR OF LOVE

*Laver*

COVENANT COMMUNITY

*Brazen altar*

PROGRESSIVE SPIRITUAL REVELATION

*Gate*

# Chapter 11

# The Altar of Incense
# "Pastor's Council"

*And thou shalt make an altar to burn incense upon: of shittim wood shalt thou make it.*

*A cubit shall be the length thereof, and a cubit the breadth thereof; foursquare shall it be: and two cubits shall be the height thereof: the horns thereof shall be of the same.*

*And thou shalt overlay it with pure gold, the top thereof, and the sides thereof round about, and the horns thereof; and thou shalt make unto it a crown of gold round about.*

*And two golden rings shalt thou make to it under the crown of it, by the two corners thereof, upon the two sides of it shalt thou make it; and they shall be for places for the staves to bear it withal.*

*And thou shalt make the staves of shittim wood, and overlay them with gold.*

*And thou shalt put it before the vail that is by the ark of the testimony, before the mercy seat that is over the testimony, where I will meet with thee.*

*And Aaron shall burn thereon sweet incense every morning: when he dresseth the lamps, he shall burn incense upon it.*

*And when Aaron lighteth the lamps at even, he shall burn incense upon it, a perpetual incense before the Lord throughout your generations.*

*Ye shall offer no strange incense thereon, nor burnt sacrifice, nor meat offering; neither shall ye pour drink offering thereon.*

*And Aaron shall make an atonement upon the horns of it once in a year with the blood of the sin offering of atonements: once in the year shall he make atonement upon it throughout your generations: it is most holy unto the Lord.*

Exodus 30:1-10

*And he made the incense altar of shittim wood: the length of it was a cubit, and the breadth of it a cubit; it was foursquare; and two cubits was the height of it; the horns thereof were of the same.*

*And he overlaid it with pure gold, both the top of it, and the sides thereof round about, and the horns of it: also he made unto it a crown of gold round about.*

*And he made two rings of gold for it under the crown thereof, by the two corners of it, upon the two sides thereof, to be places for the staves to bear it withal.*

*And he made the staves of shittim wood, and overlaid them with gold.*

*And he made the holy anointing oil, and the pure incense of sweet spices, according to the work of the apothecary.*

Exodus 37:25-29

*And the Lord said unto Moses, Take unto thee sweet spices, stacte, and onycha, and galbanum; these sweet spices with pure frankincense: of each shall there be a like weight:*

*And thou shalt make it a perfume, a confection after the art of the apothecary, tempered together, pure and holy:*

*And thou shalt beat some of it very small, and put of it before the testimony in the tabernacle of the congregation, where I will meet with thee: it shall be unto you most holy.*

*And as for the perfume which thou shalt make, ye shall not make to yourselves according to the composition thereof: it shall be unto thee holy for the Lord.*

*Whosoever shall make like unto that, to smell thereto, shall even be cut off from his people.*

Exodus 30:34-38

We are earnestly searching for the house within the house, progressing through the tabernacle (the temple) step by step, throne by throne, from one piece of furniture to another. It is imperative that we keep our focus on the deeper and more important meaning of the sanctuary, and avoid becoming overly engrossed in the physical aspects of the natural house.

Why are we searching for the dimension beyond the dimension: the cause beyond the obvious, the truth beyond the veil? We long for truth *today,* for that practical application of God's plan to change our world and personal lives now, not merely in the distant hereafter. Most of the books written about the temple or the tabernacle remind us of the types and show us their fulfillment in Christ, but many of them bypass, ignore, or openly dismiss the present practical application of these truths today. It is clear we are to follow the steps of our Master, Jesus Christ, who lived out and fulfilled the purpose of the shadows in progressive personal revelation.

> *And thou shalt make an altar to burn incense upon...*
>
> *And thou shalt overlay it with pure gold...*
>
> *And thou shalt put it before the vail that is by the ark of the testimony, before the mercy seat that is over the testimony, where I will meet with thee.*
>
> *And Aaron shall burn thereon sweet incense every morning...*
>
> *And when Aaron lighteth the lamps at even, he shall burn incense upon it, a perpetual incense before the Lord throughout your generations.*
>
> *And Aaron shall make an atonement upon the horns of it once in a year with the blood of the sin offering of atonements: once in the year shall he make atonement upon it throughout your generations: it is most holy unto the Lord.*
>
> Exodus 30:1,3,6-8,10

This has been quite a walk. We're progressing through the Tabernacle (the Temple) step by step; throne by throne, from one piece of furniture to another. But more importantly, we've been earnestly searching to discover *the house within the house.*

It is imperative that we remember not to become so engrossed in the physical surroundings of the natural house that we lose focus on the deeper and more important meaning of the sanctuary.

We are in quest of the dimension beyond the dimension: the cause beyond the obvious, the truth beyond the veil. We will press on into the house that God is building, understanding that while most epistles written about this subject remind us of the type and show us the fulfillment in Christ, many have never perceived the *present practical application* of living out the purpose of the shadows as a *progressive personal revelation.*

Our text reminds us that we are now at standing "before the veil." And here before us, directly in the center of the sanctuary next to the veil, stands the smallest of all the tabernacle furniture, the golden altar. Because of it's primary purpose of burning the incense, we know it better as the "Altar of Incense."

This altar stood three and a half feet high and was less than two feet square. But small as it was, its importance and placement in the house is indisputably pivotal.

The word for "altar" in the original Hebrew text comes from the primitive root word, *zabach,* which means to "slaughter, kill, offer as a sacrifice, and slay." This is certainly the accurate explanation for what happened at the brazen altar in the outer court, but here in the inner sanctuary, we have a totally different situation. The difference in this altar is that while the brazen altar of the outer court received the dripping blood and slimy pieces of butchered meat, all burning with a pungent and rancid smell, here at this little altar is offered the incense (*qatar*) whose definition in contrast means "a sweet fumigation in a close place thus driving out the occupants."

The smoke of the golden altar actually created such a sweetness that it was literally almost too much. Wow! Too much sweetness. Now that is different.

There was no sin offering here, those sacrifices are behind us. Here we have a beautiful type of the prayers and praises of the saints.

David himself, the preparer of the order of worship, prayed, "Let my prayer be set forth before Thee as incense; and the lifting of my hands as the evening sacrifice" (Ps. 141:2).

John the apostle, in his magnificent revelation of Jesus Christ, exploring the wonders of the glorious heavenly tabernacle of which Moses' was only the shadow, discovered this golden altar in the real house. His situation was at first, one of grief.

> *And I wept much, because no man was found worthy to open and to read the book, neither to look thereon.*
>
> *And one of the elders saith unto me, Weep not: behold, the Lion of the tribe of Juda, the Root of David, hath prevailed to open the book, and to loose the seven seals thereof.*
>
> *And I beheld, and, lo, in the midst of the throne, and of the four beasts, and in the midst of the elders, stood a Lamb as it had been slain, having seven horns and seven eyes, which are the seven Spirits of God sent forth into all the Earth.*
>
> *And He came and took the book out of the right hand of Him that sat upon the throne.*
>
> *And when He had taken the book, the four beasts and four and twenty elders fell down before the Lamb, having every one of them harps, and golden vials full of odors, which are the prayers of saints.*
>
> Revelation 5:4-8

John's tears dried as the whole company began to "sing a new song" (Rev. 5:9).

A closer look at the entrancing revelation of John continues in chapter 8 of Revelation:

*And when He had opened the seventh seal, there was silence in heaven about the space of half and hour.*

*And I saw the seven angels which stood before God; and to them were given seven trumpets.*

*And another angel came and stood at the altar, having a golden censer; and there was given unto him much incense, that he should offer it with the prayers of all saints upon the golden altar which was before the throne.*

*And the smoke of the incense, which came with the prayers of the saints, ascended up before God out of the angel's hand.*

Revelation 8:1-4

Another glimpse of this little altar from the heavenly perspective is viewed as Isaiah receives a purging of his lips with a "live coal" from off the altar. This again is the golden altar, and it seems to consistently require the participation of speech—prayers, praise, and the purging of lips!

This is the place for Words!

Here we go again...there seems to be no end to the redemption type and heavenly vision. But lo, we poor mortals dwell in this vast abyss between the shadow and the glorious tomorrow. We, here in the "now," long for a glimpse of the "hands on" application of the unseen house that God said to David would endure through every generation. There must be more to this little altar than just a spiritual application of prayer and praise. As glorious as this place of worship is, I'm still, at the risk of being thought too inquisitive and rational, looking for a "today" application of practicum.

Let me digress here to say that many of our lives have been spent in an arena of religious acceptance. We've been trained to accept the obvious. May I further state that others have given years to the constant study of this shadow, extracting truth after truth, enriching the marvelous facts concerning our redemption. But somehow, in all of our revelation and understanding, we are still constantly staggered by the simplest problems that seem to never find answers in our deepest ministerial outpourings.

Sometimes truth is so simple that we stumble over it while gazing into the heavens. Lest we wander to far afield, let us look once again in the direction of the altar of incense.

There it stands, just before the veil—the line of demarcation. The veil separates the sanctuary from the Most Holy Place. On the far side of this divider is the place of "headship"—the final height attainable in the process of growing "...up into Him in all things, which is the Head, even Christ" (Eph. 4:15). Beyond this veil is the mind of Christ, the understanding of the Spirit and the wisdom of the ages.

In the next chapter, we will discover that this glorious headship in Christ, foreshadowed in this house, is truly the place where Isaiah exclaimed, "The government shall be upon His shoulders" (Is. 9:6). We will also see that the magnificent headship in Christ has been measured unto a multi-faceted ministry bearing the hallmark of the Ascension gifts (Eph. 4:8-11).

Let me explore one more avenue in our walk past the golden altar. While we may feel we understand what the incense foreshadows and ensamples for us, let me speak briefly about it's creation and consistency.

*And the Lord said unto Moses, Take unto thee sweet spices, stacte, and onycha, and galbanum; these sweet spices with pure frankincense: of each shall there be a like weight:*

*And thou shalt make it a perfume, a confection after the art of the apothecary, tempered together, pure and holy.*

Exodus 30:34-35

The "work of the apothecary" (Ex. 37:29) was to take four sweet spices and compound them together. The incense was not a single substance. It could not be found like honey in a hive or oil in a flinty rock. Things had to be gathered and united to create the sweet aroma when poured out on the golden altar.

Now certainly, if we can learn to compound substances after the art of the apothecary, we may better know how to pray and praise. These spiritual exercises are also the putting together of various kinds of things...as Paul said, "...all prayer [all kinds of prayer] and supplication in the Spirit" (Eph. 6:18).

By the way, thank God, the veil has been "rent in twain" (Mt. 27:51), and we have access freely into the grace and mercy of God.

Now, let's look just a little closer and draw our hearts into the region of reasonable hope. As I studied the idea of compounding substances for the creation of incense, I was reminded of a Hebrew word *rigmah,* which means "to cast together stones, a pile of stones, to lapidate." The corresponding word in the Greek, *sunedrion,* means "a joint session." These words are translated into the English language as "council."

I've subtitled this chapter on the altar of incense *Pastors' Council* because I see a coming together of those lively stones (1 Pet. 2:5), the *rigmah,* the saints that praise and pray at this altar.

But I see them as *a part* of the sacrifice, willing to be compounded or brought together to create the sweet answers through purged lips. (Is. 6:7)

Remember, please, that just beyond the altar through the riven veil is the gifted ministry, containing the various facets of the nature of Christ.

One of the great tragedies of the present day church is the chasm between the pulpit and the pew. The veil seems to never have been "rent at all."

The preachers on one side formulate government with attending plans and regulations, while the congregation on the other side sits joylessly in casual obedience, waiting for the next program or presentation.

In a religious effort to negotiate correspondence between the pastor and the saint, we have created boards and committees who eventually, without purged lips or sweet spirits, made the responsibility of governing in the church a rancid, stinking mess. Our mistake is that in giving responsibility without authority or authority without submission, the wrong sacrifices end up on the wrong altars and what should have been sweetness becomes a strange and unbearable odor.

In this situation, the pastor has democratically installed controllers, and voted in resisters, while the congregation becomes a confused and embittered nest of sceptics often sitting in rebellion and anger.

We know, of course, that this old religious system is only a failed carbon copy of previously broken-down processes. On the other hand, a complete lack of governmental guidelines can be just as destructive and out of order, endangering both the ministry and the church.

I see an answer at the altar. This is, you remember, "the place for words." What if the minister could recognize the tremendous resources and wealthy deposits in the persons of his congregation? He may discover a school teacher, a machinist, a day care worker, a truck driver, a nurse, a painter, a carpenter, a salesman, a banker, or a builder. The people, although "sheep," have a certain richness and variety in their understanding of life and reality.

The pastor on the other hand, may not always be a genius, and he certainly does not contain all wisdom and skill. He is, however, almost always *afraid to admit* that he is not omniscient. At the same time, the saints rarely want to admit that he understands much more about life than they. What the pastor can do is preach and impart the precious treasures needed for spiritual success.

While the pastor certainly doesn't need a board, or the same people, making all the decisions, wouldn't it be wonderful if he could find council for the many various decisions that must be made concerning the life of the covenant community? And wouldn't it be great if a group could be gathered from the congregation with specialized understanding in various areas? There could be different groups for different decisions—builders for building, day care workers for children's ministry, mechanics for scouts, and truck drivers for transportation needs. We're not talking about creating permanent positions on never-ending committees, we're simply and briefly bringing the "government" and the "governed" together to prayerfully discuss possibilities for kingdom operations.

And by the way, we are not suggesting that talking together takes the place of prayer, or that conversation replaces worship. We simply need communication concerning the unanswered issues in the body. When this Pastor's Council is gathered, the participants would sweetly put their ideas together. This is the compounding of substances; this is also a creation of incense. The pastor is not intimidated as he listens to the needs and ideas of the congregation, and the congregation feels the unusual sense of value in their expression of thought, with different suggestions that may or may not become part of the program. The pastor (set ministry) will consider every purposed option.

When the evening is over and all the ideas assembled, a sweet aroma fills the house. Before the fire on this little golden altar goes out, the pastor, that beloved apothecary, is already thinking of another council for assistance in another area of progressive planning, and they too will fill the house with love.

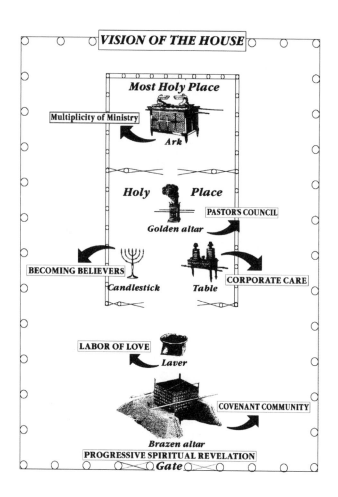

# VISION OF THE HOUSE

**Most Holy Place**

*Ark*

Multiplicity of Ministry

**Holy Place**

*Golden altar*

PASTOR'S COUNCIL

BECOMING BELIEVERS

*Candlestick*

*Table*

CORPORATE CARE

LABOR OF LOVE

*Laver*

COVENANT COMMUNITY

*Brazen altar*

PROGRESSIVE SPIRITUAL REVELATION

*Gate*

# Chapter 12

# *The Ark of the Covenant "Multiplicity of Ministry"*

*And they shall make an ark of shittim wood: two cubits and a half shall be the length thereof, and a cubit and a half the breadth thereof, and a cubit and a half the height thereof.*

*And thou shalt overlay it with pure gold, within and without shalt thou overlay it, and shalt make upon it a crown of gold round about.*

*And thou shalt cast four rings of gold for it, and put them in the four corners thereof; and two rings shall be in the one side of it, and two rings in the other side of it.*

*And thou shalt make staves of shittim wood, and overlay them with gold.*

*And thou shalt put the staves into the rings by the sides of the ark, that the ark may be borne with them.*

*The staves shall be in the rings of the ark: they shall not be taken from it.*

*And thou shalt put into the ark the testimony which I shall give thee.*

*And thou shalt make a mercy seat of pure gold: two cubits and a half shall be the length thereof, and a cubit and a half the breadth thereof.*

*And thou shalt make two cherubims of gold, of beaten work shalt thou make them, in the two ends of the mercy seat.*

*And make one cherub on the one end, and the other cherub on the other end: even of the mercy seat shall ye make the cherubims on the two ends thereof.*

*And the cherubims shall stretch forth their wings on high, covering the mercy seat with their wings, and their faces shall look one to another; toward the mercy seat shall the faces of the cherubims be.*

*And thou shalt put the mercy seat above upon the ark; and in the ark thou shalt put the testimony that I shall give thee.*

*And there I will meet with thee, and I will commune with thee from above the mercy seat, from between the two cherubims which are upon the ark of the testimony, of all things which I will give thee in commandment unto the children of Israel....*

*And Bezaleel made the ark of shittim wood: two cubits and a half was the length of it, and a cubit and a half the breadth of it, and a cubit and a half the height of it:*

*And he overlaid it with pure gold within and without, and made a crown of gold to it round about.*

*And he cast for it four rings of gold, to be set by the four corners of it; even two rings upon the one side of it, and two rings upon the other side of it.*

*And he made staves of shittim wood, and overlaid them with gold.*

*And he put the staves into the rings by the sides of the ark, to bear the ark.*

*And he made the mercy seat of pure gold: two cubits and a half was the length thereof, and one cubit and a half the breadth thereof.*

*And he made two cherubims of gold, beaten out of one piece made he them, on the two ends of the mercy seat;*

*One cherub on the end on this side, and another cherub on the other end on that side: out of the mercy seat made he the cherubims on the two ends thereof.*

*And the cherubims spread out their wings on high, and covered with their wings over the mercy seat, with their faces one to another; even to the mercy seatward were the faces of the cherubims.*

Exodus 25:10-22; 37:1-9

Finally, we have come to the third dimension of the shadow, passing through the outer court and the sanctuary. This is the place of His glory, the dwelling place of the Most High (Ex. 25:8).

The room is called the "Holiest of all" (Heb. 9:3), the Holy of Holies.

We have entered in through a huge tear, a rent in the beautiful Veil.

The queen of Sheba would have loved this Veil. She could have appreciated the blue and purple, the crimson and fine linen, to say nothing of the "cherubim thereon" (2 Chron. 3:14). I am sure, however, that although she watched Solomon ascend into the house in splendor and observed the excellence of the worshipful presentations, she probably never saw it at all. If she had, she could not have passed through, because at that time there was no access for Gentiles or queens.

This marvelous royal tapestry, hanging on four golden pillars blocked the way into the splendorous treasure vault of the house. Gorgeous as it was, the veil created an impenetrable barrier for all mankind. Only the high priest could enter once a year, and then, with blood and fear of death.

And here we stand within the veil! We were invited and welcomed by mercy and grace (Heb. 4:16).

It seems by all I've heard that this ragged split in the formidable barrier of the temple veil was created during a mighty earthquake, a tremor so devastating that it opened the graves of the patriarchs and turned the noon day into the darkness of midnight.

Others say that it was not just a natural earthquake at all, but rather a thunderous shaking of the earthly elements as legions of angels paraded by course past Golgotha, awaiting permission to suck the crucified Messiah from His tortuous nails.

Others say the power of His dying cries shook the heavens and the earth—especially the last of His utterances: "It is finished!"

I'm sure that it was not just one of these, but all of that manifested power as the Spirit of the Father departed the veil of His flesh (Heb. 10:19-20), ripping the earth and the temple veil in its violence.

It is incredible that we are able to glimpse what none of the Old Testament priests could see. We are truly beholding the Glory of God in the face of Jesus Christ (2 Cor. 4:6).

Directly ahead in the center of the Most Holy Place stands the ark of the covenant. This is the masterpiece of all the temple furniture. This gorgeous chest measuring 3¾ feet long, 2¼ feet wide, and 2¼ feet high, is overlaid with pure gold on the outside and on the inside. It has a crown of solid gold, four rings of solid gold, two golden staves, and a lid, called the mercy seat, made of a slab of solid gold. Also fashioned of solid gold and overshadowing the mercy seat were the two cherubim: "...one cherub on the one end and the other cherub on the other end..." (Ex. 25:19). Gold—the type of Deity, is everywhere. This is truly the dwelling place of the Almighty.

Again, in the first dimension of the house, everything was brass—"man things"—representing judgment against flesh and sin. In the second dimension, the sanctuary function, while being overlaid with gold, was attended by man—oil for the lamps, bread for the table, and incense for the altar.

This is the God-man participation. But as we progress into the third dimension of the house, man's works cease and the ark of the covenant becomes the sovereign dwelling place of God and God alone.

There are no sacrificial fires here—no lamps to light. The glory (*shekinah*) of the God of Israel dwelt between the cherubim. "And there I will meet with thee, and I will commune with thee from above the mercy seat, from between the two cherubims which are upon the ark of the testimony, of all things which I will give thee in commandment unto the children of Israel"(Ex. 25:22).

This is without doubt the most tantalizing and magnetic spot in the house. Libraries of spiritual information could be pulled from these portals. The Shadow here is literally bursting with revelation.

Of course, we want to explore so many of the powerful revelations; like the sovereign *third dimension*...the first, second, and third court; the Father, Son, and Holy Ghost; death, burial, and resurrection; righteousness, peace, and joy; body, soul, and spirit; the Way, the Truth, and the Life; thirty, sixty, and hundred fold; gifts, administrations, and operations; plant, water, increase; yesterday, today, and forever; grudgingly, of necessity, and cheerfully.

There are more than 100 references to the *three dimensions of grace* in the New Testament alone. "And now abideth faith, hope, and charity, these three; but the greatest of these is charity" (1 Cor. 13:13). *The third dimension is always the greatest because it is all God!* For example: *Death*, man can kill you. *Burial*, Joseph of Arimathea can bury you. *Resurrection*, only **God** can raise the dead!

We could go on and on, but the ark before us requires a little further study. We're still searching for the House that "God built, and not man." The golden rings and staves remind us that this glorious article was built to move. Remember that God has always been a "moving thing." But God also had a distinct method and plan for the ark's transportation.

One of the most interesting stories surrounding the ark of the covenant occurs after it had been stolen out of the house of God by the sons of Eli. Upon returning the ark from Philistine back to Jerusalem, the anger of the Lord was demonstrated in the death of Uzzah, who tried to steady the ark when the oxen pulling the cart stumbled. Scripture says, "God smote him there for his error..." (2 Sam. 6:7).

Obviously, the wrath of God was not "kindled" because of the ark's return, but rather that the mode or order of transport was never meant to be an ox cart. David later said, "For because ye did it not at the first, the Lord our God made a breach upon us, for that we sought Him not after the due order. So the priests and the Levites sanctified themselves to bring up the ark of the Lord God of Israel. And the children of the Levites bare the ark of God **upon their shoulders** with the staves thereon, as Moses commanded according to the Word of the Lord" (1 Chron. 15:13-15).

It sobers me when I remember that a good, well-meaning man (Uzzah) died because of the wrong order of things. As David longed to bring the Glory of God back to Zion, so we, the Divinely discontented, long to once again see the manifestation of the Glory of God. We must be able to inquire of Him and have Him speak to us, as He did to Moses from between the cherubim. How can we obey a voice we cannot hear?

The prophet spoke of a people who "...have eyes, and see not; which have ears, and hear not" (Jer. 5:21). They would actually stay within the veil and literally not behold the glory of God!

The reason for the loss of spiritual sensitivity is due to loss of Divine order. We have emphasized and married worldly systems, patterning our spiritual houses after the earthly kingdoms.

Furthermore, the ox cart of denominationalism and organized religion emits death and obstructs the moving of God's Spirit.

In our recent past experience, it seems that God allowed our personal interventions and offered limited blessing. But now, God is truly doing a NEW THING (Is. 43:18-19). While a few years ago this statement (God is doing a new thing) was just a religious "buzz word" type of phrase, God has put forth His hand against the commonly acceptable forms of man-made creations. He is calling into account the fleshly, phony, misguided ministries and churches, requiring repentance and contrition.

Many devastated churchmen are mourning the sad state of affairs in the church at large, and proclaiming great oaths against the supposed satanic forces causing the fall of certain personal ministries and empires. I am, however, convinced that the sad state of affairs is not so much satan as it is the judgment of God against a "Christianity" that is totally out of order and certainly without purposeful direction.

Again, like David, our motives may be pure and our hearts yearning to advance the kingdom cause, but there are too many houses being built that are just good ideas. There are too many borrowed ideas from too many broken cisterns.

Judgment must **first** begin at the house of God, and it is my studied and prayerful opinion that God is about to take away from us *everything He never told us to do.*

We envision our situation as being victims of the times, but the truth is that while we have majored in the mortal marching of time, God has moved in His eternal purpose, leaving so many of us behind.

There is a powerful spiritual evolution in progress. God is marching on from victory to victory and faith to faith. What once worked just doesn't work anymore. God is taking away the old that He may establish the new (Heb. 10:8-9).

As I continue to gaze upon the ark, I'm reminded of the glorious perfection required in this third dimension. The groggy "traditional" church cannot abide here. That old episcopal system would burst like old wineskins—the new wine of this remnant revival requires change, order and proper alignment to absolute biblical principles.

I am further reminded that as one writer stated, "Tradition always dies screaming." Change is difficult. But the traditions of men are "making the Word of God of none effect" (Mk. 7:7), and these traditions continue to impose ideas, techniques and methods upon us as though God Himself said to do it. We must stop blaming everything and everybody (including satan) for our ineptness. We must be realigned.

You will recall that in our last chapter we pointed out that the Holiest Place, the dwelling place of the ark and God's glory, was the foreshadowing of this headship of Christ in the true house. This is where the government would rest upon His shoulders (Is. 9:6). We also see here that the magnificent headship of Christ would be measured into a multifaceted ministry bearing the hallmark of the ascension gifts (Eph. 4).

This ark of the covenant chapter is therefore named *Multiplicity of Ministry*. What is the real meaning of this glorious dwelling place? Where is the true house that God is building?

Psalm 68:18 reads, "Thou hast ascended on high, Thou hast led captivity captive: for Thou hast received gifts for men; yea, for the rebellious also, that the Lord God might dwell among them."

In fulfillment, the New Testament passage repeating David's psalm reads,"...when He ascended up on high...and He gave some apostles; and some, prophets; and some, evangelists; and some, pastors and teachers" (Eph. 4:8a,11).

Without question the New Testament plan for transporting the glory via the multiplicity of ministry is clearly foreshadowed in the ark of the covenant.

The apostle, prophet, evangelist, pastor and teacher each have a facet of ministry necessary for the nurturing, feeding, and equipping of the supernatural Body of Christ. Our entrance into the house is often hindered by our limited understanding of the multiplicity of ministry. Just as it is impossible to sustain healthy growth and development with an imbalanced diet, it is impossible to get the whole picture of God's provision with only one or two reflections of the Person of Christ.

Psalm 68:18 revealed that the ascension (transforming) of the Messiah was a revelation of the "Lord God" who desired to dwell among us. The Ephesian passage divides the properties of the Person of Christ into a five-faceted ministry designed to make God's house whole. Obviously we cannot see the whole until all the parts are in place.

The old ox cart system that kills is distinguished by its one-man pastoral rule. The pastor is usually treated as both ox and cart. However, not one church in the 48 churches mentioned in the epistles have a "single leader" type of ministry in charge.

No one in the New Testament was ever called "pastor," and nowhere in the New Testament was this pastoral gift required to be the head of the Church.

This old out-of-order system has exhausted the average ministry and exalted the especially gifted ones.

Jethro, Moses' father-in-law, observed the efforts of Moses to counsel and direct the whole congregation of Israel and said, "The thing that thou doest is not good" (Ex. 18:17).

The ark was to be carried upon the shoulders (plural) of the priests (1 Chron. 15:13-15).

First Corinthians 14:33 and 40 states that all things must be done in order.

God told Moses to make everything according to the pattern.

This subject is, of course, much too consuming for the short amount of time left for us in this writing. However, may I beseech you to prayerfully pursue the subject of proper New Testament government and order in other manuscripts written by this author and others who understand the necessity and emergency of immediate response to proper kingdom alignment.

Only when men cease accepting the glory and humbly allow the burden of the Lord to rest upon them in the proper pattern will the skeptical eye of the world be dimmed and the light of the gospel of Christ awaken their spirits.

Only when we cease from our labor and enter into the rest of God beyond the veil (Heb. 4) will the revelation of the Word, the supply of manna, and the rod of miraculous power be loosed upon this dying generation.

Finally, let me remind you that David, looking out of his cedar home toward the tabernacle, desired to build God a house. He truly wanted to bring God up to his personal standard of living. But the Lord told David that the true house would be built by God Himself, and not by aspiring men.

Let us surrender "all the things God never told us to do" and sit down at the feet of Jesus, as once more He declares, "upon this rock **I will build My Church**!"

# **D** *Destiny Image*
## New Releases

### DIGGING THE WELLS OF REVIVAL
*by Lou Engle.*
Did you know that just beneath your feet are deep wells of revival? God is calling us today to unstop the wells and reclaim the spiritual inheritance of our nation, declares Lou Engle. As part of the pastoral staff at Harvest Rock Church and founder of its "24-Hour House of Prayer," he has experienced firsthand the importance of knowing and praying over our spiritual heritage. Let's renew covenant with God, reclaim our glorious roots, and believe for the greatest revival the world has ever known!
ISBN 0-7684-2015-6 $9.99p

### ANOINTED OR ANNOYING?
*by Ken Gott.*
Don't miss out on the powerful move of God that is in the earth today! When you encounter God's Presence in revival, you have a choice—accept it or reject it; become anointed or annoying! Ken Gott, former pastor of Sunderland Christian Centre and now head of Revival Now! International Ministries, calls you to examine your own heart and motives for pursuing God's anointing, and challenges you to walk a life of obedience!
ISBN 0-7684-1003-7 $9.99p

### THE HIDDEN POWER OF PRAYER AND FASTING
*by Mahesh Chavda.*
How do you react when overwhelming defeat stares you in the eye? What do you do when faced with insurmountable odds? God has provided a way to turn certain defeat into awesome victory—through prayer and fasting! An international evangelist and the senior pastor of All Nations Church in Charlotte, North Carolina, Mahesh Chavda has seen firsthand the power of God released through a lifestyle of prayer and fasting. Here he shares from decades of personal experience and scriptural study principles and practical tips about fasting and praying. This book will inspire you to tap into God's power and change your life, your city, and your nation!
ISBN 0-7684-2017-2 $9.99p

### WHEN GOD STRIKES THE MATCH
*by Dr. Harvey R. Brown, Jr.*
A noted preacher, college administrator, and father of an "all-American" family—what more could a man want? But when God struck the match that set Harvey Brown ablaze, it ignited a passion for holiness and renewal in his heart that led him into a head-on encounter with the consuming fire of God.
ISBN 0-7684-1000-2 $9.99p

## **Available at your local Christian bookstore.**

### Internet: http://www.reapernet.com